D ... ... N
THE ... U?

CLAIRE ... ...ked at
NFER-NELS... ...arched
and develop... ...adults.
Claire also ha... ...cal test
batterie... ...part of
Harcourt International). She has written two previous books, *The Potential Pack*
and *Are You Smarter Than You Think?*, which is the third title in the Penguin
Compass series of books on self-discovery.

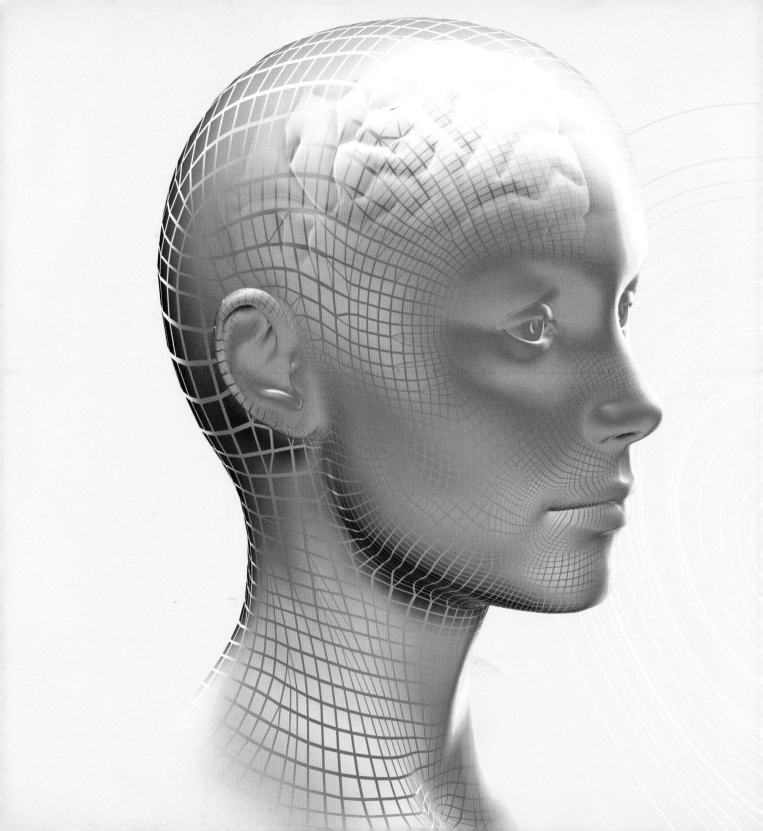

DO YOU KNOW
THE REAL YOU?

More Than 66 Ways to Understand Your Personality

CLAIRE GORDON

PENGUIN
COMPASS

PENGUIN BOOKS
Published by the Penguin Group
Penguin Group (USA) Inc., 375 Hudson Street, New York,
New York 10014, U.S.A.
Penguin Group (Canada), 90 Eglinton Avenue East, Suite 700, Toronto, Ontario,
Canada M4P 2Y3 (a division of Pearson Penguin Canada Inc.)
Penguin Books Ltd, 80 Strand, London WC2R 0RL, England
Penguin Ireland, 25 St Stephen's Green, Dublin 2, Ireland
(a division of Penguin Books Ltd)
Penguin Group (Australia), 250 Camberwell Road, Camberwell, Victoria 3124,
Australia (a division of Pearson Australia Group Pty Ltd)
Penguin Books India Pvt Ltd, 11 Community Centre, Panchsheel Park,
New Delhi – 110 017, India
Penguin Books (NZ), cnr Airborne and Rosedale Roads, Albany, Auckland 1310,
New Zealand (a division of Pearson New Zealand Ltd)
Penguin Books (South Africa) (Pty) Ltd, 24 Sturdee Avenue, Rosebank,
Johannesburg 2196, South Africa

Penguin Books Ltd, Registered Offices:
80 Strand, London WC2R 0RL, England

First published in Great Britain by Carroll & Brown Limited 2005
Published in Penguin Books 2005

1 3 5 7 9 10 8 6 4 2

CARROLL & BROWN LIMITED
20 Lonsdale Road London NW6 6RD

Text copyright © Serif Limited, 2005
Compilation copyright © Carroll & Brown Limited, 2005
All rights reserved

CIP data available
ISBN 0-14-219639-8

Printed in Singapore

CONTENTS

WHAT IS PERSONALITY?

Commonly used in everyday language to describe someone's mental identity, personality describes the way a person thinks, acts, and feels. We say, for example, someone has "bags of personality," or is "a real personality" if he is she is extravert, eccentric, or charismatic. But, for psychologists, personality also has a special and technical meaning.

One of the most important ways in which psychology differs from the natural sciences arises from the existence of individual differences. Two molecules of water that are treated identically react in exactly the same way, but any two human beings, even identical twins, may respond quite differently when someone, for example, steals their parking space. All water looks the same, but people differ from one another not only in their appearance but also in their behavior, or psychologically. Psychologists have searched, and are still searching, for ways of explaining these differences between people. They also want to know how does personality come about. Are we born with our personalities? And what factors influence how our personalities develop?

First-time parents are often surprised that their baby seems to have such a strong personality so early in life, and they are even more surprised when they have a second child who is very different from the first. These reflections are supported by research, which shows that children as young as three months have distinctive personality characteristics. In fact, twin studies (of identical, fraternal, and twins raised apart) indicate that much of personality is genetic – you are born with many of the elements of your personality, which are inherited from your parents. Certain traits, such as sociability, and emotional stability, are particularly influenced by genetics. That being said, however, genetic factors only account for about half of your adult personality.

So what else makes you what you are? Well, your environment, for one. Adults who formed secure attachments to their primary caregivers in their first year of life have been found to approach problems with persistence and enthusiasm, to be self-directed, eager to learn, and to be social leaders amongst their peers. Conversely, children who do not form secure

attachments are more dependent on other adults, more easily frustrated, and tend to be socially withdrawn.

Parenting style is crucial during childhood: Some parents are warm, nurturing, and child-centered; others are more occupied with their own lives, highly controlling, indulgent, or rejecting. These styles shape a child's personality. Authoritarian parenting, for example, tends to lead to children who are less sociable and lack spontaneity.

There are a few problems with evaluating the role of environmental factors in personality. The first is that there is a "chicken-and-egg'" element: Sociable parents may pass their "sociable" genes on to their children, but they also create a sociable environment at home, with plenty of opportunities for children to develop their social skills. Another problem is that it is quite common for each parent to have a different parenting style, or for parents to employ different styles in different situations. Parents may treat a son differently from a daughter, or the "baby" of the family differently from older siblings. Humans are very complicated!

Your cultural background also may impact on your personality. Western cultures prize responsibility, motivation to achieve, and independence, and praise confidence and assertiveness in children. Yet 100 years ago, children were "seen and not heard." Many non-Western cultures place value on the interdependence of children, rather than independence, and encourage children to be part of the community rather than to compete and do better than others. Different cultures put a premium on different personality traits, which impacts on parenting styles and a child's personality development.

It can be an interesting exercise to think about what factors may have shaped who you are today.

PERSONALITY AND AGE

When you look back over your life, you can probably pick out elements of your personality that have stayed pretty consistent: Perhaps you have always been a bit shy, or like being in control, or are a perfectionist. At the same time, you can probably think of ways you have changed: Perhaps you are less impulsive than you used to be, or are better at getting along with people. Sometimes these changes can be attributed to life events: Going to college, having children, losing a partner.

It's commonly thought that by the time you reach 30, your personality is set in stone. Research suggests that not only do people continue to change after this milestone, but in some ways they change more.

What's the theory?
It is believed that we typically develop our personality type – our preferred way of doing things – throughout the course of our lives in response to our surroundings and experiences. However, it isn't always possible to live your life in a way that suits your personality: A loud and noisy schoolchild will have to behave in a more introverted and controlled way in the classroom. An introverted manager who would rather work alone will need to interact with other people in the office.

As middle age approaches, the dominant behaviors from our personality may begin to seem boring and less obvious or underused aspects of our personality may emerge. This experience is common and may result in a so-called "midlife crisis" – the cliché of the quiet businessman who buys a motorbike and fashionable clothes, or the woman who starts dating younger men and going to night clubs. But some people just don't feel the need to nurture previously hibernating personality traits. Everyone is different.

Researchers in the United States have found, however, that all people's personalities change as they age, and in more subtle ways – in fact, they mellow. Conscientiousness and agreeableness increases throughout life and particularly during one's 20s and 30s. This means people become more organized and self-disciplined, and warmer, more generous, and helpful. These changes coincide with starting a family and the subsequent responsibilities that come with that particular life experience.

What does it mean for me?
The personality changes associated with age generally take place over a long period of time. These changes are probably heavily influenced by the environment you live in and what happens to you throughout your life. If you accept the premise that your personality shifts with age, then it follows that you have the opportunity, over a lifetime, to make your own minor adjustments to your personality if there are elements you feel disadvantage you. You can work at being more discreet if you reveal secrets easily, or set out to provide emotional stability for your children if you feel you lack it.

Do you feel you have mellowed since childhood? What about your peer group or your siblings? You can explore this issue with friends or family. Your parents have the insight of knowing your personality as a child. How do they feel you have changed, if at all?

The enneagram is a dynamic way of representing personality. Its nine points form into three groups of three. Each group denotes a particular orientation – feeling, sensing, and thinking, and there are three different types in each one. Every person has all nine characteristics, and through time, we normally progress through each group though some of us "get stuck."

The aspects of sensing personality are known as "judge" and "helper" with some "peacemaker and "narcissist". Feeling includes "artist" and "observer" with some "hero" and "narcissist." Thinking is represented by "opportunist" and "chief" with some "peacemaker and "hero."

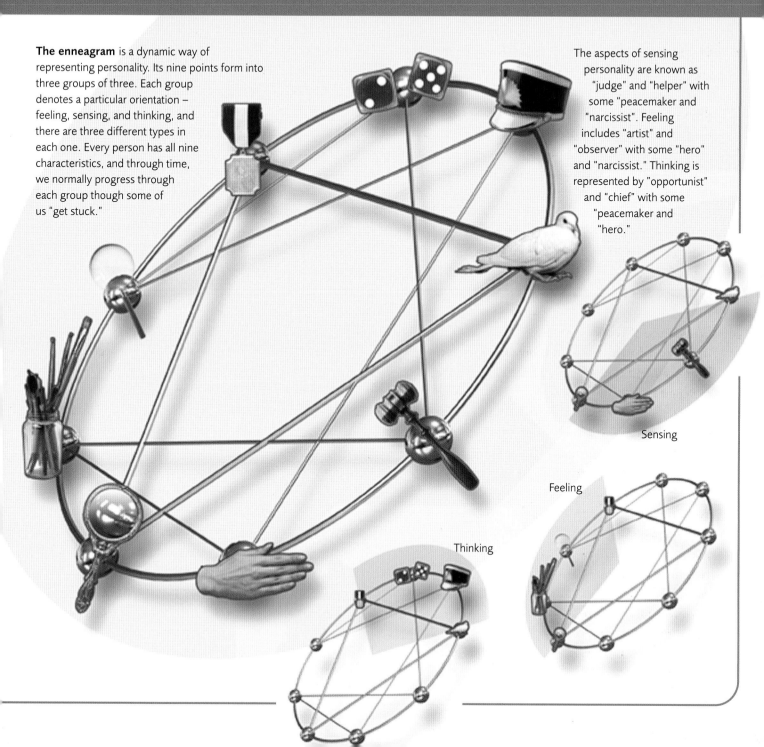

Sensing

Feeling

Thinking

PERSONALITY AND BIRTH ORDER

For many years, psychologists have studied the way children develop behavior patterns, ways of thinking, and emotional responses. There are many structures and theories for explaining a child's personality development, and one of these is birth order. There is significant anecdotal evidence, academic research, and plain common sense to suggest that your place in your family influences your personality. According to research from Concordia University, Montreal, only sex has a stronger influence on personality traits than birth order.

In fact, researchers go on to suggest that the traits developed from order of birth are so pronounced that they can be tapped to make highly efficient sales tools, with firstborns being more susceptible to brand names and celebrity endorsements and later-borns being more open to new innovations such as internet banking.

Your birth order helps determine your expectations, your strategies for dealing with other people, and your own weaknesses.

What's the theory?

Birth order is characterized as: Only child or firstborn, middle child (or children), and lastborn. Researchers believe that there are common characteristics to these birth places, although the dynamics within families can change relationships and these should be considered equally. The variables that affect each family situation include the number of years between children, the gender of the child, physical differences, disabilities, the birth order position of parents, any blending of two or more families due to death or divorce, and the relationship between parents.

Only child or firstborn

Only children or firstborns tend to be motivated achievers with high aspirations. They stick to rules, are more competitive, and natural leaders. They can be bossy, perfectionist, and forceful characters. Their drive, determination, and attention to detail, together with an innate sense of entitlement, means that the worlds of politics and management are full of firstborn children.

Of the first twenty-three astronauts sent into outer space, twenty-one were firstborns or only children.

Middle child (or children)

A good description of a middle child is a diplomatic peace-maker. Middle children are good mediators and have superior cooperation skills: They don't have their parents all to themselves or always get their own way, so they have to learn to negotiate and compromise. They enjoy being part of a group or team, and often make excellent managers and team leaders because of their skills. They can be too eager to be liked, however, and find it difficult to set boundaries. They also tend to blame themselves when others fail.

Lastborn

Youngest children in the family are typically outgoing and great at motivating other people. They are also affectionate, fun, warm, uncomplicated, and sometimes a little absentminded because they have had the least responsibility within the family. Lastborns tend to get bored quickly and can be a bit self-centered. Studies show that the baby of the family gravitates toward vocations that are people-oriented. Good sales people are often lastborns.

What can birth order mean to me?

There are no magical formulae to help us understand our friends and family. However, birth order research offers clues about why people tend to be the way they are. With a little self-analysis, you may gain insights into your own behavior. Think about your place in the family and how it may be affecting you. For example, if you are a middle child, you may find arguments very unsettling because your natural tendency is to placate warring parties, as you did with your siblings as a child.

Birth order placement can help you know what to expect of others, what to avoid, and how to get the responses you want. This can be an advantage in parenting, teaching, sales, and other occupations. Knowing an individual's birth order position can help to give clues to understanding why an employee behaves the way he or she does and to predicting how someone might react in particular circumstances. Lastborns, for example, may flourish in a nurturing environment, rather than an aggressively competitive one. The older brother of sisters could be an effective manager of an all-female department.

If you have children, think about how their birth order and the dynamics of the family may be influencing their personalities. Try to offer them experiences that counter the more negative aspects of their birth order. Encourage a firstborn to negotiate rather than dominate, ask a middle child for his or her opinions and views, give the lastborn specific responsibilities in the home.

Multiple personality is the existence of two or more integrated and well-developed personalities within the same individual. In most cases, each personality has his or her own name, age, memories, life story, and physical and behavioral characteristics – all in the same body. It's not uncommon to hear someone referred to as having "a Jekyll-and-Hyde personality" – a reference to the well-known character(s) in R.L. Stevenson's book. Often, each personality has no awareness of the experiences of the other or others. Periods of unexplained memory loss for hours or days are a clue to the presence of multiple personalities.

While the Jekyll-and-Hyde scenario is an extreme example, the phenomenon of multiple personality is more likely to manifest as follows. Take as an example a man in his 20s. His name is John and this is his primary personality – the person he is most of the time. John is shy and polite. John's multiple personalities are Peter, Bruno, and Max; they all coexist with John and can take over from him. Peter is consensual and kind. Bruno is a nine-year-old boy who cries a lot. Max is aggressive, cold, and angry, and protects John in dangerous situations. John speaks, acts, behaves, dresses, and even walks differently depending on which of his personalities is the current dominant one.

What's the theory?

People with multiple personalities suffer Dissociative Identity Disorder (DID), which means that the person has two or more distinct identities that regularly take control of his or her behavior and consciousness. Dissociation is the disconnection from full awareness of self, time, and/or external circumstances. Sufferers are relatively few and far between, but there are enough cases for psychologists to have studied them.

No one claims to know for sure what causes DID, but it seems that childhood trauma – physical, emotional, or sexual – may play a part. The explanation is that to cope with extreme distress, a child's unconscious mind creates an alter personality with characteristics that can cope with the abuse, and that this new imaginary personality shields the "real" child from reality. Children do have fantastic imaginations, and pretend play is a natural part of childhood. However, if this strategy continues into adulthood, these identities become very real and permanent. If abuse continues, more personalities may be created, and each one will take on a life of its own.

The treatment for DID is psychotherapy or "talk therapy," with a view to combining the personalities back into one. This type of therapy is very time-consuming; it can take a number of years. Moreover, the therapy has variable success rates. Once aware of their multiple personalities, patients can communicate directly with them and get used to them. However, the very idea of integration – the cure – can be resisted by the patients. They seem to need the multiple personalities and fear losing them, and of course the abuse or trauma that generated the alter identities in the first instance has to be faced up to and dealt with, which is usually extremely painful for the individual.

What can multiple personality theory mean to me?
Try to imagine what it must be like to have another personality coexisting in your body, taking over and talking to your friends and family, doing your job, or making decisions about your life. It's so hard to fathom, isn't it? But dissociation exists along a continuum from normal everyday experiences to disorders that interfere with everyday functioning. I can guarantee that you have dissociated at some time in your life.

Have you ever driven a familiar route, say your journey to and from work, or to your parents' home and realized you can't remember a portion of the journey? This is sometimes called "highway hypnosis," and is a trancelike feeling that develops as the miles go by. Or what about when you are reading a book or watching a movie and you slip into a sort of daydream, realizing as you come to that you haven't taken in the plot, read the words, or heard the dialogue? Researchers and clinicians believe that dissociation is common and natural. Like so many mental illnesses, DID stems from a normal activity that has become distorted.

Personality is the combination of traits, types, and the emotional or behavioral preferences with which you are born. Or is it? Would you like to be more intelligent, popular, sexier, confident, and less shy? Major drug companies are working on a range of pharmaceuticals that can achieve just that; Prozac was the first drug users felt changed their personalities – they felt more confident, more optimistic about the future, and saw their self-esteems rise. Would you like to run faster, lift heavier weights, or train more effectively? So-called "performance-enhancing drugs," like anabolic steroids, are used (albeit illegally) by a minority of athletes and sports people across the globe. The reported side effects include personality changes, such as increased aggression and decreased empathy.

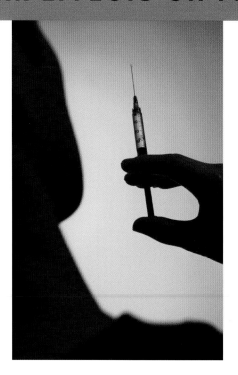

Throughout history, people have taken mind-altering drugs for a variety of reasons: To prevent tiredness on a hunting trip, or to communicate with their gods using hallucinogens. South American tribes have a Medicine Man, whose incredible knowledge of plants is used to treat a wide range of symptoms, including the psychological or emotional. There are many drugs available today – illegal, prescription, and over-the-counter – which have the ability to influence personality. Some people positively seek these changes; for others they are just a side effect.

What's the theory?

There are four main categories of drugs which impact on our psyches and personalities. The first are "lifestyle" drugs, of which Prozac is a good example. Prozac was developed as a new generation antidepressant, to help people feel less fearful, more outgoing, and more self-confident. The difficulty with lifestyle drugs is that we instinctively fear that the majority of users are trying to cosmetically improve the "normal," rather than benefiting from a cure for a life-affecting problem or illness.

The second category is performance-enhancing drugs, taken by sports people to improve their ability in the gym, pool, track, or field. Most of these drugs work on developing muscle tone and strength using derivatives or equivalents to the male steroid hormone, testosterone. The condition "roid rage" occurs when people taking steroids become overly aggressive, and this personality change persists while the drug is being taken. It is an unwanted side effect.

So-called "recreational" drugs form the third category of mind-altering drugs; examples include cannabis, LSD, cocaine, even alcohol. These are normally taken specifically for the purpose of changing the user's reality or personality. People report increased libido, easygoingness, humor, open-mindedness, and a feeling of real connection with other people, but the effects are pretty short-term. The social and personal negative impact of these drugs has been widely discussed in the media.

The final category is conventional medicines used to treat psychological and psychiatric disorders. These have been developed by drug companies to control and change undesirable symptoms of mental illness, and as such to change the patient's personality in some way. They are available on prescription only, and may be administered in a medical setting or in the community.

What could drug-taking mean to me?

The two areas where people positively seek to change their personalities are lifestyle drugs and recreational drugs. The junction of personality and pharmaceuticals in these life choices throws up a number of ethical issues. Consider these questions:

- Is personality a natural gift that shouldn't be tampered with?
- Would you change your personality by popping a pill if you could?
- Isn't it normal to be depressed when someone close to you dies; to be anxious about certain social situations; to be unhappy when relationships fail?
- What's the difference between cosmetic surgery and lifestyle drugs?

Perhaps the strongest argument against changing our personalities with drugs is that of diversity. Variety is the spice of life and we find interaction and relationships with others stimulating because of our different personalities. Even more importantly, diversity is essential for the evolutional survival of our species. Some of us are naturally braver than intelligent, more caring than confident, more reflective than impulsive, more sensitive than charming. Evolutionally speaking, we need the brave to fight, the cautious to warn, the intelligent to plan, and the sensitive to care for us. Diversity and the ability to adapt to the changing environment are paramount in the success of any species.

CULTS AND PERSONALITY

The Concise Oxford Dictionary defines a cult as "a system of religious worship; devotion, homage to person or thing." Nowadays, the word "cult" is more likely to be associated with brainwashing, manipulation of followers, public scandals, murder and mass suicide, rather than religious worship. Some well-known examples and events probably spring to mind: The tragedy in Waco, Texas where 75 people died in a siege of the Branch Davidians, a breakaway sect from the Seventh-Day Adventist Church led by David Koresh; "Jonestown" and the 918 people who died in 1978 following the order of Jim Jones to drink cyanide-laced "Kool-Aid;" and the still-active Unification Church, known as the "Moonies" after their leader Sun Myung Moon.

The role of psychology and personality is central to cults. At the core of a cult is its founder leader: A self-appointed "Messiah" who is authoritarian and unaccountable, but charismatic, enigmatic, and captivating. Cult members tend to have certain personality traits in common, too. Psychological coercion is used to recruit, indoctrinate, and retain followers, and gradually their personalities and behaviors are altered to suit the cult.

What's the theory?

A key characteristic of cults is that they are built on the "cult of personality" of a seemingly charming and charismatic leader, usually male. He sets up a hierarchy of close associates of a similar personality and inclinations and uses it to demand total obedience from followers through heavy punishments often with a strong psychological element. Personal relationships are governed by the leader of the cult on the basis of the excessive authority he is granted based on his messianic or prophetic pretensions. He decides who will be friends with whom and who will have sexual relations with whom and often especially with him – a great honor. Clearly the personality of the leader is incredibly magnetic and persuasive for members to follow him in this way.

Members become obsessed by the cult. It becomes the most important thing in their lives. Cult members often give up their families, jobs, and homes to join the cult, where every aspect of their lives is controlled by

they are idealistic, and seek self-knowledge and self-improvement. They want to make a difference in life, and believe life should have a meaning and purpose. They want to love and be loved, to feel special, influential, recognized, and accepted. These psychological needs may be acknowledged by the individual but it is more likely they are not. A common feeling on meeting a sympathetic group is that "this is exactly right," or "this is what I have been looking for" and feeling no doubt. The more un-met needs a person has, the more powerful the attraction and adherence to the group, and the more difficult it is to leave.

What can cults mean to me?
We can learn a great deal about our society, our leaders, and ourselves from thinking about cults. Can you think of historical political leaders who were malevolent or benevolent examples of the "cult of personality?" Adolf Hitler? Winston Churchill? Mahatma Gandhi? What psychological techniques did they use? Think about leaders in the wider sense, too: Religious, educational, moral, media owners, multinational corporations. How are they influencing you; what effect do they have on what you think or feel, or how you act or behave?

The likelihood of you being at risk of joining a cult is very small, but think about the psychological needs that define you as a person and influence your personality. Are these needs being met? Explore ways of addressing these needs which are self-empowering, rather subjecting yourself to the power of others.

their leader. They usually have to prove their dedication by giving almost all their money and possessions and much of their expertise and time to the cult. Sometimes they pursue careers to help the cult, giving their expertise and their earnings willingly to the organization.

There are lots of myths about cult members, and the sort of people they are. They actually come from all walks of life, and are all ages. The most likely cult recruits are from an economically sound family background, have average or above intelligence, and a good education. The common personality factor is that

Personality is made up of thoughts, emotions, and behaviors, which together define your personal style and influence your interactions with others. The study of personality is the oldest field of psychology; in 400 BC Hippocrates recognized four basic personality types – melancholic, choleric, sanguine, and phlegmatic. About 100 years later, Theophrastus, Aristotle's successor as head of the Lyceum in Athens, proposed that there were 30 personality types, each with a different character's name (such as "the liar," and "the flatterer"). In the 1940s an American doctor called William Sheldon developed the theory of somatotypes based on body physiques – endomorphs, ectomorphs, and mesomorphs.

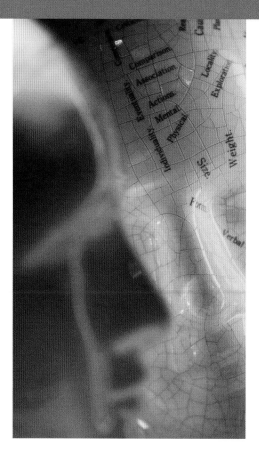

continuum. These theories are more complex, difficult to measure, and interpret, but their complexity is believed to make them accurate. Different psychologists have come up with scales, such as that for "boldness" or "empathy." A person is rated according to how much of that trait he or she possesses. So, at one end of the scale, would be a person who is adventurous and takes risks, while at the other end, would be someone who is cautious and holds back a bit. Both extremes might be needed in different occupations or organizations but there isn't much call for a risk-taking lawyer, or a cautious stunt person!

Types versus traits
Personality-type theories, such as the above, propose that people can be categorized into discrete types. The simplicity of this approach is both appealing and limiting. It does help us get a fix on personality in an immediately useful and understandable way, but in labeling people as types, it overlooks the undoubtedly more complex aspects of each individual.

Personality trait theories, on the other hand, propose that people's individual personality features are on a

Benefits of personality testing
Until the 1960s, personality testing remained of clinical and research interest only. Today, however, personality testing is available to everyone, and can give valuable insights into our mental makeup, particularly if the results are interpreted and communicated to us by a psychologist or someone skilled in testing. By learning what sort of roles and organizations fit best with your natural temperament, you can help your career development. By gaining knowledge about your own

motivations, strengths, and weaknesses, you can achieve personal growth and development.

The biggest growth by far in personality testing is now in the workplace, for pre-employment selection, and employee and team development. Imagine you are a business owner, wanting to get the best out of your people. You can try such things as training and development, mentoring, coaching, and employee-assistance programs, but if an employee's values and behavior don't fit with the rest of the organization and its culture, you may have problems that could impact on the entire workplace.

You also may want to recruit a particular type of person for a specific role. Sales people, for example, need to enjoy working on their own if they are on the road for long periods of time. Project managers need to be able to encourage and motivate team members, while having an overview of progress toward an immovable completion date.

So far, we've talked about types and traits, and what you can get out of understanding your own personality. There is another way of categorizing facets of personality, both types and traits.

Internal types and traits are relevant to how you as a person think and feel, your motivations and desires. It is important to understand these facets because knowing yourself will help you understand others. Do you find it difficult to keep motivated on a project? Do you believe in keeping to and following rules?

External types and traits are about how you relate to others, and your interactions with colleagues, partners, and friends. Have you ever just not hit it off with someone, and find he or she grates on you? Have you ever met someone new, and felt you both just gelled – as if you'd known each other for ages? That is the power of personality!

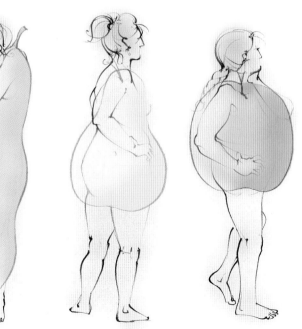

Somatotypes

These are descriptions of personality based on body shape and first described by Dr. William Sheldon. Endomorphs, who are plump and buxom, are relaxed and sociable; mesomorphs, who are muscular, are active and assertive; ectomorphs, who are lean and delicate, are quiet and sensitive. Today, body shapes are mainly used to predict a person's long-term health – pear- and bean-shaped individuals are healthier than apples!

Personality testing is a fact of modern life, with an estimated 2500 tests in use worldwide. The majority of corporations use personality tests as part of their hiring, promotion, and team-building process and they are also used in custody battles, college entrance exams, and in sentencing and parole decisions. They are used by individuals in search of self-knowledge – the reason you are reading this book in the first place! It is important therefore that you know who uses these tests, why they are being used, what types of personality tests there are, and how you, the test-taker, can benefit from them.

Who uses tests and why

It is increasingly common now for organizations to use psychological tests as ways of finding out more about potential employees. Tests aid fair recruitment if an "ideal" personality profile is established before candidate testing starts, as they provide a level playing field by which everyone's results can be compared.

Each individual is unique, yet all individuals have similarities and these may have important consequences. If you are employing technicians to visit customers in their workplaces, your

technicians must be good at talking to new people and enjoy working independently. If you are looking for new senior managers, they must be socially confident, and good at motivating staff. Tests are also used with current employees. Many companies have a policy of filling vacancies internally, and anyone applying for a promotion may be asked to take a personality test to see how he or she corresponds to the personality profile of the new job. Project teams made up of cross-department working style members, are commonly created to tackle specific organizational issues. The role of personality in building a successful team is well-researched and testing is carried out for this purpose.

Tests also are used in schools and colleges to assess students. Initially, tests may form part of the selection process, and later on they are used for career guidance. They help students to better understand their strengths and weaknesses so that they can make more informed choices about which occupation to enter. In common with careers guidance testing, a third use of tests is to promote adult self-understanding. You may want to know why you find some things easy and other things difficult, why you prefer to work or learn in a certain way, and what your talents are so that you can maximize them.

Types of tests

There are standard methods of gauging just how sophisticated tests are, and tests which reach these exacting standards are called professional psychological tests. These should be the only tests used by professionals in schools, colleges, and organizations, because they have been proved to be valid (they measure what they say they measure), reliable (the results can be depended upon and are stable over time),

and fair (the tests do not discriminate against any gender, race, or creed).

Every country has a professional body for psychologists that governs the use of psychological tests. In the United States, this is the American Psychological Association. The APA has guidelines about the restricted sale, use, and interpretation of psychological tests. The general public cannot buy or have access to professional psychological tests because their administration and interpretation requires specialist psychological training. This also ensures that no candidate has seen the items before the testing session.

The tests in this book are based on professional psychological tests, but have been written so that they are self-rated. This means you can explore aspects of your personality without worrying about the outcome, because you don't have to share your answers with anyone else. Although they aren't professional tests, you will still find them fun, interesting, and insightful.

Getting the most out of tests

Taking the tests in this book will help you clarify your view of yourself and to develop and achieve personal growth. If you do not recognize yourself in the test results, check what other people think by asking friends, family, bosses, peers, and the people who work for you. Bear in mind that personality tests do not measure the whole you: Your talents, interests, values, and life experiences also contribute to making you the person you are.

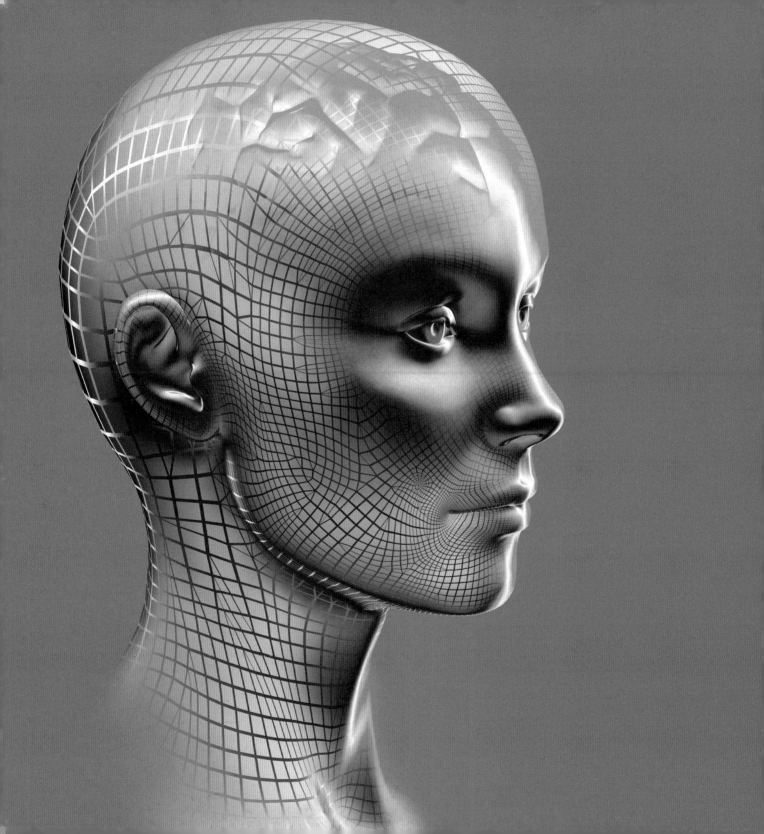

PART 1

INTERNAL
TRAITS

WHAT ARE INTERNAL TRAITS?

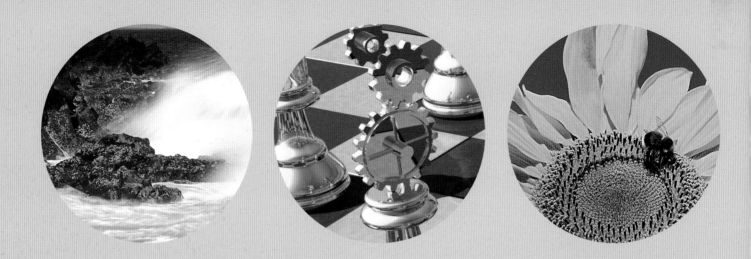

One of the ways we categorize personality is to break it down into "traits" – individual features of personality that are possessed to a greater or lesser degree. We may describe ourselves or others as "dominant," "sensitive," or "warm," and by doing so, we are identifying consistencies in behavior, and anticipating how we will respond to particular situations. This gives us some security in predicting someone else's reactions or behaviors – we can prepare a response in advance or try to change an event to avoid the predicted outcome. You would, for example, need to handle a sensitive child gently if a favorite toy was broken by another child or you might rehearse a confrontation with a dominant work colleague to ensure you have the opportunity to put your point across.

The most direct way of assessing how much of a particular trait someone possesses is to ask the person! In practice, this is done in a form of a structured interview; the same questions are asked of each person, and the answers are usually given in a form, which can be scored easily. A test may measure just one trait (as in this book) or several traits simultaneously.

Test developers compose questions that best represent each trait. To test dominance, for example, one of the questions you might be asked is "Do you like to be in control at all times?" If you answer "Yes" to the question you would be scored as "dominant." Traits, however, are judged on a continuum, or sliding scale, and the opposite of "dominant" is "deferential." Therefore, if you answer "No" to the above question, you would be scored as "deferential." At the end of the test, your position on the dominant-deferential continuum would be determined by the number of "dominant" scores as opposed to the number of "deferential" scores.

Some of the most well-known personality tests in the world are based on traits and take this approach. One of these is the 16PF® questionnaire, developed by Raymond Cattell. His research into the measurements of

personality came up with 16 basic traits, and he devised a questionnaire to measure these, called the Sixteen Personality Factor Questionnaire (or 16PF for short). Another personality questionnaire is the Minnesota Multiphasic Personality Inventory (or the MMPI). Rather than rating themselves, test-takers answer "true," "false," or "cannot say," to a series of statements about attitudes, symptoms, and past experience. The MMPI questionnaire was originally developed for clinical use, but its use has since extended to the general population.

This chapter contains tests that measure your internal traits, those relevant to how you think and feel, and what motivates and drives you. Make sure you read through the test instructions carefully, but don't spend too long thinking of an answer or the correct response – the first thing that comes into your mind is usually the most accurate.

You may want to consider whether you are taking the test for self-knowledge or as preparation for a job. Many people think and behave differently at home than they do at work; generally a person's "at home" persona is his or her true self, and a person's "work" persona reflects how he or she would like others to see him or her. You might, for example, be a very discreet person at work, revealing little about your private life or feelings, but at home with friends and family, you may openly express your thoughts and emotions.

Exploring your internal traits will help you understand more about yourself, your motivations and talents. What are your drives and motivations?

Please note: This chapter contains simplified personality tests based on personality trait theory. It is not a replacement for the full 16PF® or MMPI questionnaire or any other professional personality test, and the results are not intended to be the psychometric or practical equivalent to 16PF® or MMPI questionnaire results.

ARE YOU WARM OR COOL?

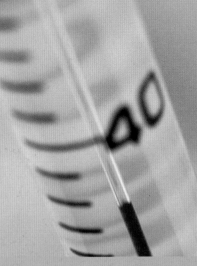

Temperature is measured in degrees along a continuum. Just as the mercury on a thermometer will rise or fall as you battle with a fever, so, too, can personality be measured in terms of warmth and coolness. And, just like temperature in other contexts, there are times when heat is an advantage, and times when coolness is preferred.

Warm people are friendly, outgoing, sociable, empathetic, and attentive to others. They enjoy closeness with other people, and seek out and maintain friendships. They are good at jobs that involve relationship building, such as nursing, project management, or public relations, and make caring and generous life partners.

TEST YOUR TEMPERATURE

Due to heat conduction, or transfer ability of materials, some objects feel cold to the touch, others seem neutral, while some actually seem warm. This is due to the way the object reacts to the heat from your hand: if it conducts heat your body warmth is quickly dissipated through the object and it feels cold; if it is a poor conductor, the heat from your hand remains almost exactly where you are touching the object so it feels warm.

Reflect on the images of the different materials shown or, if you can, find objects made from these materials in your home or outdoors

that you can touch. Think about how they feel when you touch them, and what sort of personality each would be if it was a person. Which one best reflects your personality?

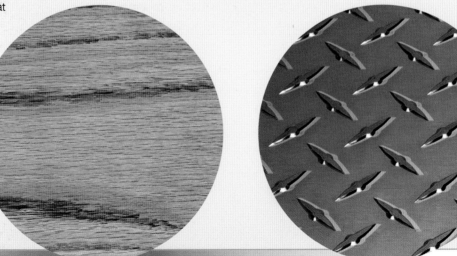

A downside of a warm personality is its gullibility. And another drawback is that others can find the warmth and care a little smothering.

People with cool dispositions are reserved and cautious by nature, and don't get carried away with extremes of emotions. Cool people are comfortable being on their own, and enjoy solitude. Their detachment means they are good at jobs that require introspection or can be done alone. They are also good at making difficult and emotional decisions. Really cool people may verge on coldness, "freezing" people out, and feeling uncomfortable if they have to spend too long in the company of others.

SCORING/INTERPRETATION

Wood is organic and reflects back heat. If you choose wood – you are a warm individual.

Metal is shiny, hard, and disperses warmth before it becomes too hot. If you like metal – you are a cool type.

Stone is neither hot nor cold. If you pick stone – you are lukewarm.

If you are warm by nature, you'll know that you need lots of people around you, both friends in your private life, and a job that involves teamwork. Your danger zone is an over-reliance on others for your self-esteem and emotional security. Try to build in some time on your own to nourish yourself from within.

If you are cool, you are emotionally self-sufficient. You enjoy hobbies you can get absorbed in, but this is often to the exclusion of other people or activities. Spending too much leisure time alone can lead to "rusty" social skills, so try to interact with other people in a social environment. You may seem distant to others, so remember to smile!

If you are lukewarm, you can probably achieve a good balance between emotional warmth and coolness. A great skill is to be able to switch from one to the other depending on the circumstances. You might want to show your warm side with your friends or partner, and your cool side when returning a damaged or faulty item to a store.

WHAT'S YOUR THINKING STYLE?

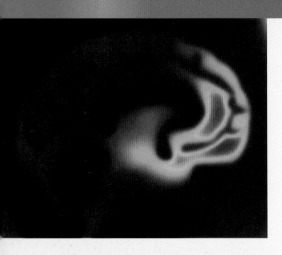

When we think through a problem, different parts of our brain become involved. The left side of your brain focuses on detail and analysis, the right side produces lateral and creative thinking. Often, one side dominates a person's thinking style, manifesting itself as a preference for either analytical or creative thinking. Analytical or logical thinking starts with a problem, and through a sequence of organized thoughts that follow on from each other, you arrive at a solution. If you are a creative thinker, the process is more free flowing; you look at a problem from lots of different angles.

If you have high left-brain activity, you are highly logical. You solve problems by seeking out information and facts before making solid decisions.

TEST YOUR LOGICAL/CREATIVE MIND

Your approach to logic and creativity will reflect itself in your surroundings. Imagine you were given a choice of these three wallpapers. Which of these patterns appeals to you most – and why?

Pattern A, right
Pattern B, middle
Pattern C, far right

You probably enjoy numerical problem solving, and are good with data. Your weakness is that you resist trying out new ideas, and may stifle creativity by evaluating ideas before they are fully formed.

If you have high right-brain activity, your thinking is more creative. You solve problems innovatively, and can come up with lots of solutions to a problem. You also prefer to make decisions on the basis of opinions, feelings, and "hunches," rather than lots of numbers. Your weakness is that you get bored with detail, and often want to rush ahead. You may also tend to let your heart rule, rather than your head.

SCORING/INTERPRETATION

Logical people tend to prefer ordered and regular patterns, while creative types appreciate more chaotic and abstract backdrops.

Pattern A is random and imaginative. If you choose A – you are a creative type.

Pattern B has free-flowing elements merged with more regular images. If you like B – you are center-brained.

Pattern C is ordered and highly structured. If you select C – you are a logical type.

If you are creative, try to follow things through even if you get frustrated, and give your left-brain neurons a chance to network. Discipline your thinking by making decisions in a series of steps. For practice, try breaking down an everyday activity into stages: write down instructions for someone making his or her first cup of coffee.

If you are center-brained, both sides of your brain are working equally. You solve problems flexibly and can apply either an analytical or creative approach. Your weakness is that you may not be analytical or creative enough in certain situations. Try consciously using one approach and then the other to ensure the full benefit of both thinking styles.

If you are a logical person, try to hold back your natural desire to analyze, and allow your right brain some free rein. Make yourself explore all the options before marching on toward a solution. Try a brainstorming activity, writing down as many choices as you can.

ARE YOUR EMOTIONS UNDER CONTROL?

Do you find yourself reacting to life's events against your better judgment? Do external factors affect your moods? Or, perhaps you have the ability to control your emotions, staying outwardly calm and unruffled, despite the storm raging around you.

People with lower levels of emotional stability tend to feel a lack of control over life's challenges and to "react" to life rather than adapting or making proactive decisions – thus "reactivity" is the key element in emotional stability. Whereas for most people reactivity simply reflects current life challenges (such as a new baby or a new job, situations in which nearly everyone tends to feel less in control and more emotionally vulnerable), for emotionally reactive people, reactivity is part of how they live their lives, buffeted from one stressful life event to another. Emotionally reactive people can be easily upset and somewhat temperamental. The plus side is that a positive event will invoke enthusiasm and joy in this individual, which can be infectious.

Emotionally stable people are calm, mature, and unruffled. They feel that life is more-or-less in their control. They tend to take things in their stride, and to cope with day-to-day life and its challenges in a calm and balanced way. They can adapt to frustrations, and don't let their emotions get in the way. However, the downside is that emotionally stable people may be uncomfortable with "negative" feelings, such as anger, jealousy, and sadness, and either keep them suppressed or deny their existence. A degree of emotional self-expression is important for mental well-being.

TEST YOUR REACTIVITY

Read through these questions, and answer each with a "yes" or "no" response:

Do you:

1. Find that other people say that they find you very even-tempered?
2. Like planning your free time so that you can look forward to events?
3. Sometimes wish you could experience the emotional highs and lows that others seem to?
4. Try not to think about your emotions too much?
5. Find it difficult to lose your temper?
6. Feel in control of your life?
7. Wish that people would keep their emotions in check?
8. Find that people turn to you in times of crisis?
9. Get accused of being emotionally cold or repressed?
10. Usually feel calm and unstressed?

SCORING/INTERPRETATION

If you answered yes to 7 or more of the questions – you are emotionally stable.
If you answered yes to 3 or less of the questions – you are emotionally reactive.
If you answered yes to between 4 and 6 of the questions – you are balancing emotions.

If you are emotionally stable, you think through your actions carefully, and keep your emotions in check. However, your stability may be because you have built up defenses around yourself that may not be altogether healthy. Make sure you are not denying emotions – although there are times when it isn't appropriate to express your feelings, ignoring them isn't healthy either.

If you are emotionally reactive, you live and die by your feelings, wearing your heart on your sleeve, which can make others wary of you. You are probably great company when in a good mood, but difficult to pull out of a bad mood. Try to develop an element of emotional stability – continual buffeting by life's stressors will wear you down.

If you are balancing emotions, is it because you veer from one extreme to the other? Stable at work, but reactive in your personal life; or mainly stable, but with moments of reactivity? In any event, you need to identify and control the trigger factors that lead to reactivity.

HOW DO YOU REACT TO SITUATIONS?

We have all come across dominant personalities: People who take control in social situations, making it quite clear to all how they are feeling, what they want to do, and how they want things done. There are undoubtedly times when this is exactly what is needed, and dominant people make efficient organizers. On the other hand, there are times when this hard-nosed approach tramples over other people's feelings and wishes, and then dominant people can seem overbearing, argumentative, and difficult.

What about deferential personalities? These are easygoing people, who usually agree with everyone to avoid tension or conflict, even if it means

TEST YOUR DOMINANCE QUOTIENT

You are going to use some of your childhood memories to explore your personality type: dominant or deferential. Spend a few moments thinking back to access memories of arguments and disagreements in your family.

1. How did you resolve disagreements with your siblings?
(a) I would normally call in one of my parents as an arbitrator.
(b) Eventually I couldn't be bothered, and would walk away.
(c) I had to win, and would fight to the bitter end.

2. Were your parents dominant or deferential?
(a) dominant
(b) deferential
(c) one parent was dominant, the other deferential

3. What were your coping strategies for upsetting events?
(a) To avoid arguments or displays of emotion if possible.
(b) To cry – it helped to release the tension.
(c) To take it out on someone.

4. What was your family's approach to life?
(a) Taught to respect each other's feelings and stand up for ourselves.
(b) Easygoing, seldom fought, and would never "clear the air."
(c) We said what we thought, and competed to be in control.

suppressing what they really think. They are consummate cooperators, accommodating individual differences selflessly. Deferential types are pleasant and easy to be around, and put others before themselves. However, all this altruism can be a bit wearing when you need an honest opinion, or when a confrontation is unavoidable.

Dominant or deferential behavior is often developed in childhood as a result of parenting styles or sibling rivalry. As a result, a third personality style is often taught in personal development workshops or management training courses: assertiveness. Assertive behavior is that which clearly conveys what you want, while at the same time recognizing and respecting the rights of others. Assertive individuals tend to achieve much more in the long run, both personally and professionally.

Note down your memories, thoughts, and interpretations. Can you "see" influences in your childhood that have helped shape your adult personality? Are you deferential, dominant, or assertive (somewhere in the middle)?

SCORING/INTERPRETATION

1. (a) 1 (b) 0 (c) 2
2. (a) 2 (b) 0 (c) 1
3. (a) 0 (b) 1 (c) 2
4. (a) 1 (b) 0 (c) 2

Add up your total score.
If you scored 6 or more, you are a dominant type.
If you scored 2 or less, you are a deferential type.
If you scored between 3 and 5, you are an assertive type.

If you are a dominant individual, you are a strong character who tends to take command. You are probably competitive, and may like a good argument. Your danger zones are aggressive tendencies, which can generate conflict, break down goodwill, and damage relationships. Work on developing warmth in your relationships. Aim to be assertive rather than aggressive.

If you are deferential, you tend to put others before yourself in all respects, making you a thoughtful friend and a conscientious worker. However, there are two danger zones here: first, ignoring your own needs may sap your confidence; second, extreme deference can be annoying. Remember: if you are asked for your opinion, the chances are the other person really wants to hear it!

If you are assertive, you neither seek nor shirk conflict, and respect others as much as you respect yourself. Think about the times you have conceded, and the times you have dug your heels in. Did the outcome benefit you?

STAR ATTRACTION OR SUPPORTING ROLE?

Our relationships with others are like a glorious bouquet of flowers in which a balance of shapes, colors, and textures – in this case personalities – combine to produce a harmonious, pleasing arrangement.

Some of us like to be center stage and are colorful, lively, and high spirited, just like exotic blooms forming the focal point of an arrangement. Many entertainers or media personalities fit this description. These lively people are carefree, enthusiastic and spontaneous, and great fun at social gatherings or when you need cheering up. However, they can be impulsive and unreliable, and may benefit from friends with a calming influence.

Other individuals are more like foliage, a foil for the flowers. These types are more serious, careful, and quiet, and are a stabilizing and mature influence on livelier friends. They make reliable and loyal friends, and are good at jobs that involve dedication to routine or repetitive tasks. At the extreme, however, they can come across as a little dull, and emotionally flat. They need lively people around them to keep their spirits up and encourage their *joie de vivre*.

TEST YOUR LIVELINESS QUOTIENT

Look at these pictures and think about each plant's visual characteristics and use in a formal floral arrangement. Which one best reflects your personality?

If you are a lively person, you'll thrive on being the center of attention in all types of social situations. You're probably the life of the party when on top form! Your danger zone is that you find it difficult to rein in your enthusiasm when a little decorum is called for, and you may say or do things that upset or embarrass others. Try some techniques to bring yourself down from your "highs;" count to 10 before you crack a joke, or practice deep breathing to calm you down.

If you are more serious, you'll enjoy spending your time in quieter, more contemplative activities. Your cautious nature makes you think everything through carefully. But, you need to develop a little spontaneity to open up your life to new experiences, and help you grow as a person. Challenge your routine: replace your usual morning cappuccino with something new from the coffee menu, or book a holiday somewhere you've never been before.

If you are equable, you know when restraint is called for, and when you can let your hair down. Liveliness is associated with youth, and we all become a little more restrained as we get older and become more mature. If you are a parent, you can rediscover the joys of spontaneity and impulsivity through your child, remembering to teach him or her when more thoughtful and quiet behavior is appropriate.

SCORING/INTERPRETATION

Sunflowers are exotic and exuberant blooms around which an eye-catching arrangement can be built. If you choose the sunflower – you are a lively person.

Subtle and supportive foliage, like ferns, frame flowers, allowing them to be displayed to maximum effect. If you opt for the fern – you are a more serious person.

Pretty flowers, like roses, can complement a showier one, like the sunflower, but don't strive to be the star of a bouquet. If you select the bunch of roses – you are equable.

REBEL OR CONFORMIST?

Rules are regulations, procedures, or customs laid down for us to follow. They can be religious ("thou shall not commit murder"), legal (speeding limits), organizational (no smoking allowed in the office), or social (greetings on meeting someone). Attitudes to rules vary between cultures. Some cultures have lots of rules that are obeyed by all members; in others, the rules are there but also an accepted norm about which are breakable.

Attitudes to rules vary between individuals, too. At one extreme are those people who conform to rules and are bound by them. They are dutiful, scrupulous, proper, and conscientious, and accept and promote conventional cultural standards. Rule-conscious types are law-abiding citizens and excel at jobs where there is a clear structure to be followed, such as law enforcement or the legal profession. The downside is that they can come across to other people as inflexible, moralistic, or self-righteous.

At the other extreme, lie the rule-breakers. They don't worry about conventions, obligations, or following rules and regulations. They are non-conforming and expedient, and use whatever means possible to get the job done. They are often the mavericks within an organization, or excel at self-employment where there are no externally set rules. They can be fun to be around, but extreme types irritate the more rule-conscious, and breaking rules can be troublesome or plain unlawful.

TEST YOUR ATTITUDE TO RULES

Take a look at these two images. Assign each of these adjectives to either the pirate or the naval officer:

Official	Self-driven	Loyal
Unconventional	Respectful	Alternative
Compliant	Rigid-thinking	Fickle
Rebellious	Flexible	Obedient

Now read through the adjective list you've drawn up for each image. Think about your own attitudes to rules. Would you rather be a pirate, or in the navy?

If you are a rule-breaker, you'll believe that rules are there to be challenged, and shouldn't be followed without thinking. You're likely to be a free spirit, and non-conforming in your life choices, appearance, or way of thinking. However, lawlessness could get you into trouble. Have you fewer internalized standards, or maybe you simply have unconventional values. Are you a rebel to make a point to someone?

If you are rule-conscious, you'll believe in order and that regulations serve an important purpose. You are likely to be conventional and tidy in appearance and attitudes. However, you need to guard against rigidity in your thinking and behavior – development thrives on a degree of free thinking. Ask yourself whether your attitudes originate from your upbringing or from experiencing misfortune as a result of not following rules, or perhaps from rules providing comfort and security?

If you are a rule-chooser, you have probably learned the rules you need to follow. Watch out that your rule-consciousness and rule-breaking are appropriate and properly considered. Social rules are generally more fluid than organizational rules, for example. When are you rule-breaking? Is it with certain friends or in particular situations?

SCORING/INTERPRETATION

Steve Jobs, the co-founder of Apple Computers, said in 1982, "It's more fun to be a pirate than to join the navy." Pirates are the ultimate rule-breakers, whose achievements result from their ability to work and live "outside of the box." The Navy, on the other hand, succeeds through rule-obeying, and this sort of tight, ordered, predictable structure affords security to both the individual sailor and the nation the Navy serves.

If you see yourself as a pirate, you're a rule-breaker.
If you prefer the Navy, you are rule-conscious.
If you can see bits of yourself in both images, you are a rule-chooser.

SHY OR BOLD, WHAT'S YOUR STYLE?

Think of the word *bold* and one of the following may come to mind: bright, brassy colors; an intrepid explorer; someone who speaks his or her mind plainly; or even a **bold** font on your computer. The common factor is something standing out, making an impact.

Boldness can also be applied to social situations. Socially bold types are outgoing and confident. They don't fear rejection, so feel comfortable initiating social interactions and are at ease in new or daunting social settings – for these reasons, they make great sales professionals and journalists. To others, they can seem somewhat intimidating, as they are strong personalities who, for better or worse, cannot be ignored. If they also

TEST YOUR SOCIAL STRATEGY

In chess, the goal of each player is to attack his/her opponent's King so that it has no escape (called "Checkmate"). Chess pieces are symbolic of a medieval society, and include a King and Queen (the monarchy), Bishops (the church), and Pawns (the foot soldiers).

The pieces all move in different ways, and can be said to have different personalities, strengths, and weaknesses. The King can move one space in any direction. The Queen can move any number of spaces in a straight line, in any direction, even diagonally. Bishops can only move diagonally, but as little or as far

as you want. Pawns can move forward one space, although they can take another piece by moving forward diagonally.

Look at this portion of a chess game. The King is in Checkmate: every space around him is equally dangerous. If he moves into spaces 1, 2, or 3, he will still be in the direct line of the Queen. She is all-powerful, audacious, and confident, and can move swiftly and lethally around the board. If the King moves into space 4, he will be in

exhibit warmth and liveliness, bold people will be fun to be around and they help others relax in difficult situations.

Socially shy people are quite timid and easily embarrassed. They find public speaking a nightmare, and don't enjoy large social gatherings where striking up conversation with strangers is required. They are more likely to fear the unknown rather than embrace it, so are much happier with routine and the company of familiar faces. They are easily threatened and may withdraw from difficult social situations rather than have to go through with them. However, these gentle people may be sensitive listeners, who pick up subtle social clues from watching by the sidelines.

Checkmate from the black Pawn. Pawns are uncomplicated and straightforward pieces; their strength is in numbers, and they work better in teams because they are weak in isolation. If the King moves into space 5, he is in the direct line of an attacking Bishop; remember, they attack sideways only. They are rather aloof and shy pieces, who remain on the sidelines until called into action. They are also seen as somewhat sly or crafty.

Think about the personalities and roles of the Queen, Bishop, and Pawn. Which one are you?

SCORING/INTERPRETATION

If you are like the Queen – confident, charismatic, and in control – you are socially bold.

If you are like the Bishop – waiting on the sidelines, standing back from the action – you are socially shy.

If you are like the Pawn – straightforward, more secure within your own group – you are a balance of bold and shy, or socially cautious.

If you are socially bold, you probably have a wide circle of friends, and enjoy meeting new people. Speaking to large groups doesn't intimidate you. Your danger zone is that you can appear thick-skinned, over-bearing, and attention-seeking. Try toning down your voice, keeping your body language relaxed, and making sure you listen to and take a genuine interest in others.

If you are socially shy, you will undoubtedly avoid most social gatherings and holidays where meeting other people is part of the fun. You probably don't complain about bad service. Your danger zone is that others will find you aloof. People who observe rather than take part are viewed a little suspiciously. Don't let yourself become socially isolated.

If you are socially cautious, you'll enjoy meeting people as long as you have some friends around you, or are "in the mood." Perhaps you find socializing difficult, but make an effort as part of your job, or for your partner. Wariness of strangers is natural, but at times it is unnecessary.

WHAT'S YOUR HUMOR?

In ancient Greece, most people believed that diseases were sent as punishments from the gods, and treatments were aimed at pleasing the gods rather than relieving the symptoms and eliminating the causes. Hippocrates, the Greek doctor and philosopher, went against this conventional thinking. He looked on the body as having a balance between four humors – sanguine, choleric, melancholic, and phlegmatic. If a person was ill, it meant that there was an imbalance in his or her humors and he or she should be treated to return the balance back to normal. His search for symptoms became the foundation of modern medicine.

The concept of humors has been embraced and developed over time, and has come to be applied to temperament, an aspect of personality. Temperament reflects the emotional moods most often prevalent in us. It provides a backdrop to our emotions, and influences the way we interpret events and our responses to them. There is strong evidence, both scientific and anecdotal,

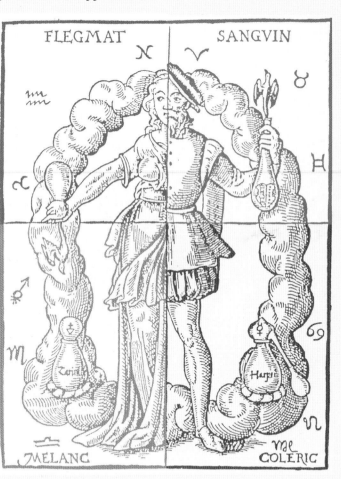

that temperament is something we are born with. Ask any mother about her baby's temperament, and she will describe it accurately and in detail.

What can can identifying my humor mean to me?
People are a mix of more than one humor but those those that are diametrically opposed – phlegmatic and choleric and sanguine and melancholic are rarely found in one person. Generally, you will have characteristics of the temperaments that bound your essential core humor. If you are a melancholic, you will also have traces of the phlegmatic and choleric. Ideally, you want to be in balance with an integrated personality. This can be achieved by letting more of the qualities of the most favorable of your supporting humors have greater precedence. For melancholics, this should be their choleric sides; for cholerics, their melancholic parts; for phlegmatics, their sanguine natures, and for sanguine individiuals, their phlegmatic tendencies.

Phlegmatic personalities are careful, passive, and even-tempered. If you are phlegmatic, your strengths are your carefulness, calm and perseverance. Your weaknesses are your shyness and dislike of change. Your calmness can be a great stabilizing influence but you can frustrate others if you "switch off" when you need to get involved. You'll enjoy routine and the familiar, so challenge yourself by trying something new.

Sanguine types are usually outgoing, easygoing, and adaptable. If you are sanguine, your strengths are your sociability, eloquence, and friendliness. Your weaknesses are your lack of attention to detail and impatience. Your fun-loving nature is an asset, until you face situations that require depth and reflection. You'll enjoy a lively and fulfilling social life – try to include some thought-provoking activities in your schedule.

PHLEGMATIC
Aloof, nonchalant, thoughtful, careful, calm, detached, peaceable, affable

SANGUINE
Responsive, cheerful, talkative, optimistic, extrovert, lively, forgetful

MELANCHOLIC
Pessimistic, reserved, quiet, unsociable, brooding, sober, thoughtful

CHOLERIC
Excitable, impulsive, restless, energetic, noisy, heroic, impatient, angry, intolerant

Melancholics are more reserved, thoughtful, and sober in their approach to life. If you are melancholic, your strengths are your intellect, thoughtfulness, and powers of observation. Your weaknesses are your pessimism and reserve. Your sensitivity can be used constructively when you reach out to other people, but if that same sensitivity is turned back on yourself it can erode your self-esteem. You'll enjoy lively discussions with friends, so try keeping a conversation lively and upbeat.

Choleric people are described as impulsive, excitable, and energetic. If you are choleric, your strengths are your energy, stamina, and extroversion. Your weaknesses are your intolerance and forcefulness. You have the ability to set goals and follow them through, but you need to be careful to take others with you in your vision. You'll enjoy outdoor activities and sport, so try some team games where you aren't the leader.

ARE YOUR FEELINGS TO THE FORE?

Your body uses its five senses to inform your brain about what is dangerous, safe, or pleasurable. At times, a person's body can be overly sensitive to physical stimuli – a smell that is offensive, noise painful to the ears, for example – are quite common complaints.

But what about emotional stimuli? Our brains react to these, too, but here the situations involve other people rather than objects or the environment. Sensitive personalities are in tune with their feelings, and tend to view the world from this perspective. They are intuitive and sentimental, and love a "weepy" movie. They are kind, and their warmth and empathy make them sympathetic and attuned to other's feelings. Extreme sensitivity,

TEST YOUR REACTIONS

Water is one of our natural resources and can take many forms. Look at these images and note down your immediate thoughts and to which aspects of the images you are drawn.

however, can lead to too much subjectivity and not enough focus on the facts. This can result in some sensitive souls overlooking the practical aspects of a project or the advantages of taking an objective perspective on a situation.

There are others who are definitely not ruled by their feelings or anybody else's – sappy movies are their worst nightmare! These unsentimental folks are realistic, logical, no-nonsense, and self-reliant. They focus more on how things work than on aesthetics or refined sensibilities, and are concerned with utility and objectivity. There are times when this is an advantage, particularly in a heated disagreement, but because these people don't tend to admit or accept vulnerability, they may get into trouble in situations that demand awareness of feelings.

SCORING/INTERPRETATION

If you focused on the purpose of the water, the waterfall as a hydro-electric power source, the waves might cause a flood, the glass of water as a drink, the rain as a life-force for plant and animals – you are an unsentimental type.

If you focused on the beauty of water in nature, or emotions the images evoked, the rainbow in the waterfall, the sun sparkling through the glass, the pattern of the raindrops – you are a sensitive soul.

If your focus varied from image to image, you are sense aware.

If you are unsentimental, your feet are firmly planted in the here and now. You will be objective, tough-minded, and matter-of-fact, and probably have a rational way of thinking that isn't swayed by emotions. You are good at cutting through arguments and getting to the heart of a matter, and would be good at a job where a cool head is needed in times of emotional stress, such as the rescue services or social work. Your potential weakness is that you don't allow for the human factor in your decisions – this is particularly important in your private relationships. Try to develop empathy by mentally role-playing a scenario before you speak, and anticipating another's reactions.

If you are a sensitive soul, you'll enjoy aesthetic and refined pleasures that arouse and stimulate your senses – culture, the arts, dining out and fine wine, and good conversation. You probably are known as a good listener by your friends or colleagues, and are comfortable talking about your feelings with other people. You would be particularly suited to a job in the caring professions, such as nursing or therapy. Your weakness is an over-reliance on the use of feelings in decision-making. Sometimes you will need to take an unpopular or upsetting decision, but you have the necessary skills to communicate your reasons to others in a sensitive and understanding way.

If you are sense aware, you'll fall into one of two types. Either your sensitivity is reserved for one sphere of your life (there are lots of ruthless business people who are dedicated and loving partners and parents), or you are genuinely neither sensitive nor unsentimental. Think about which of these types is true for you.

DO YOU TRUST OTHERS?

Are people inherently good and trustworthy, or do you wonder what their motives are? Your attitudes to trust are shaped by both your innate personality, and the environment in which you were brought up. Families tend to have philosophies about life, which parents pass down to their children. Were you taught to be wary and cautious of others, or were you taught to expect good in them? Your beliefs about encounters and interactions with other people, particularly those you don't know intimately, has a strong influence on your personality in this respect.

Trusting people tend to be easygoing and expect fair treatment and good intentions from others. They are unsuspecting, forgiving, and accepting, and expect to have reciprocal relationships. They are easy to be around and deal with; they don't bear grudges or take offence, and view people at face value.

TEST YOUR ABILITY TO READ EXPRESSIONS

The human face has the ability to make dozens of expressions, which we learn to read or interpret at an early age. Usually a combination of the eyes, forehead, and mouth are used to communicate our intentions to others.

Look at these faces. Make a note of what you believe each person is feeling or thinking.

They risk being taken advantage of by others because they are naïve, and they can also be sensitive to being misunderstood.

Vigilant people tend to notice other people's motives and intentions, and are canny at picking up body language cues and thinking about what drives the other person. They then use this information to act or speak accordingly. The positive side to this approach is that they are streetwise, and are rarely tricked or manipulated by others. The downside is that such people can be suspicious, distrustful, and wary, which can lead to all sorts of relationships getting off to a bad start. It's very difficult to recover trust that has been broken.

SCORING/INTERPRETATION

Do you believe person 1 is (a) happy or (b) pretending to be happy or friendly?

Do you believe person 2 is (a) shy or (b) feeling guilty about something?

Do you believe person 3 is (a) thinking about something or (b) plotting or scheming?

If you chose a's you trust other's easily.

If you chose b's you are vigilant.

If you chose a mixture of a's and b's, you are tentative.

If you trust others easily, you will tend to seek out new relationships and acquaintances, believing that good things will happen and you have nothing to lose and everything to gain. This optimism will normally be repaid, but there will be times when you don't see the whole picture – not everyone is as straightforward and open as you, and you will need to look under the surface to explore people's true feelings and motivations. While trust is crucial with a partner, it is less critical in working or casual relationships.

If you are vigilant, you will be skilled at interpreting other people's desires, fears, and motivations, even when they are implied. You notice body language, voice inflection, and facial expressions, and put this information together with your previous experiences of interactions with the person and your knowledge about them. If you use these skills carefully, you are able to engineer "win-win" situations. However, in your personal and intimate relationships, you need to be able to relax your vigilance, because at the extreme your mistrust may feel like animosity to those close to you.

If you are tentative, aim for trust at home and mild vigilance at work or in casual social situations. The ability to switch modes is important, so consciously put yourself into the appropriate frame of mind. Being vigilant is quite tiring, so relax into a trusting environment when you can.

ARE YOU EARTH- OR HEAVEN-BOUND?

Are you someone who focuses on what is practical and real and happening right now? Are you the sort of person who concentrates on detail, and feels most comfortable with concrete facts and figures? Earth-bound types, like you, are great project managers, and are brilliant at organizing social or community events because they think through all the practical minutiae. Their weakness is in "not seeing the wood for the trees;" they get so absorbed in sorting out the details that they can't see the bigger picture.

Perhaps you're more attracted to things and ideas still to be discovered or explored. You are more oriented to abstract ideas than to external facts and practicalities. Imaginative and contemplative, abstract types like you love ideas, possibilities, and theories. They excel at creative jobs, and their approach to life often has an outlet in their personal life through hobbies and

interests such as interior design, fashion, and writing. The risk is that they can be so absorbed in their own thoughts that they come across as absentminded and impractical.

WHICH VIEW ARE YOU DRAWN TO?

Your approach to this personality type can be explored through views and landscapes. Look at this scene. Which part of the view are you drawn to? What emotions are aroused in you? If you could place yourself anywhere in this picture, where would it be?

If you are heaven-bound, you love the idea of opportunity and possibilities. You'll probably enjoy debating theories and discussing ideas with friends. Your thinking isn't limited by what you know, and you look outward and upward for inspiration. Your strengths lie in imagining possible solutions to problems, so you might enjoy a job where creative problem-solving or idea-generation is the focus, such as advertising or marketing. However, you are not good at anticipating practicalities, and you move on quickly to other things when you get bored. Try following through just one of your ideas to its logical conclusion.

If you are earth-bound, you are better at working on a specific solution to an issue, rather than thinking up lots of unusual ways of doing something. The sorts of jobs where you would be in demand include journalism or medicine, where you need to focus on the facts and commit to a particular course of action. You can be unimaginative or too literal because your method of thinking is so concrete. Try changing your daily routine in one small way, and be open to the opportunities it might bring.

If you are horizon-bound, you are a solid mix of being down-to-earth, and able to switch modes into fantasy and abstractedness. Maybe you are an efficient manager, at home or at work, but enjoy the arts. Maybe you are a great storyteller, or have a good eye for design. There will be some way in which your heaven-bound nature is expressing itself.

SCORING/INTERPRETATION

If you found yourself drawn to the winding path or the mountains in the distance, you are heaven-bound.

If you found yourself drawn to the stream and its immediate surroundings, you are earth-bound.

If you found yourself drawn to the cottage and paddock, you are horizon-bound.

ARE YOU EASY TO READ?

Discretion is not only "the better part of valor," but also a much respected trait in courtiers and diplomats. Celebrities, too, look for absolute discretion in their employees so they can protect them from press intrusion into their private lives. So discretion is appreciated by others, but how does it manifest itself as a personality trait?

Discreet people are private and non-disclosing. They tend to be guarded and reluctant to disclose personal details, and "play their hands close to their chests." They are the sort of people who can be difficult to get to know; they must trust you before they will open up, and may be reluctant to reveal any sort of intimate information. However, they are reliable and sensitive.

Then there are people whose personality is forthright, self-revealing, and open. They are willing to talk about themselves readily, even about fairly personal matters. They tend to "put all their cards on the table," and to be genuine and unguarded. There is seldom any confusion or misinterpretation of conversations or decisions taken. Because you are drawn in by their easy disclosure, you may feel emotionally closer to them than you are in reality.

TEST YOUR PLANET AFFINITY

The planets get their name from the Ancient Greek "planetos," which means wanderers; and our knowledge of each planet in our solar system varies tremendously.

We know most about our own planet, Earth. We live on it and we explore it. Volcanic activity has even revealed a great deal about its core and space exploration has allowed us to view it from space. Earth has revealed many of its secrets to us.

Mercury is the planet nearest the sun, from which it never wanders far and as such is nearly always in the sun's glare. It is too near our blinding and scorching sun to make surface exploration possible, despite a rocky surface similar to our Moon. Astronomers

If you are open, your probably feel at ease with most people and believe in honesty as the best policy. You are transparent to those around you, because you talk about issues and events quite openly. You can come across as too self-disclosing, making others feel uncomfortable with your revelations and confessions; another risk is that you may be forthright in situations where it might be more astute to be circumspect or tactful. Think carefully before revealing things about yourself or others. What will the impact of your information be?

If you are discreet, you probably have a few very close relationships, although you may have a number of social acquaintances. Discreet people value discretion in others; when you do talk about yourself you expect the information to be treated in confidence. You may come across as aloof or unfriendly and difficult to get to know. Try widening your circle of trust a little. As a general rule, if someone reveals something to you, you will become closer by responding in a similar way.

If you are tactful, you probably strike the right balance between openness and discretion. Do you consider the best approach before speaking? Do you tend to show one trait in some situation or with some people more than others? There are times when each style yields the best results.

were unable to access it until recently but there are some areas of the planet that have never been seen.

Venus, halfway between Earth and Mercury, is the brightest planet in the night sky. It was long believed to be Earth's heavenly twin, since it is nearly identical in size to Earth, and is our planetary neighbor. During the 18th century, astronomers thought the dark and bright patches on the surface of Venus were landscapes, but in the 1960s, robot exploration revealed these were actually 20-mile-thick clouds that hid a completely inhospitable surface. Venus is not all it seems.

SCORING/INTERPRETATION

If you are like Earth – easy to get to know and revealing – you are open.

If you are like Mercury – keeping parts of yourself hidden from others – you are discreet.

If you are like Venus – appearing straightforward but retaining some privacy – you are tactful.

WHAT'S YOUR COLOR?

Color has always played a crucial role in nature. Animals and insects instinctively know that some colors mean "Don't eat me, I'm poisonous!" and that other colors say "Come and get me!" Color is used by bees and wasps to warn off birds and small mammals, whereas bees and butterflies find flowers as beautiful and beguiling as we do. Their attraction to a particular plant ensures its fertilization and seeds for the next generation.

But what is color? When light from the sun passes through a prism, the light is split into the seven visible colors, those of the rainbow. Color therapy, the use of color to change and brighten our moods, is also known as light therapy for this reason. Light is a form of energy, which is why certain colors can stimulate spiritual or emotional rejuvenation.

Color has a profound effect on humans at all levels: physical, mental, emotional, and spiritual. For example, solace can be found in nature's soothing greens of trees and plants while excitement is generated by brightly colored neon signs. We are surrounded by color now in ways that would baffle and overwhelm earlier generations: extraordinary palettes of paint and dye for our homes, cars, and clothes; color televisions and computer screens. We use color every day of our lives without even appreciating it, from reading traffic signals to identifying ripe fruit.

One of the most influential works on the psychology of color comes from Dr. Max Lüscher, a German who created the Lüscher Color Test in 1948. Lüscher bases his test on eight colors, each carefully chosen because of its particular psychological and physiological meaning.

The theory goes that if colors generate emotional responses and associations, then the colors people prefer could say something about their current emotional status and personality.

As a result of Lüscher's research, color is now being used in very positive ways: by businesses to ensure employees work more productively; by hospitals to soothe and restore patients to health, and by schools to create a learning atmosphere. Our understanding of the benefits of light and color is growing all the time.

Gray The color of neutrality, gray communicates an element of non-involvement or concealment. It's a color that remains uncommitted and uninvolved.

Blue This is the color of calmness, repose and unity, symbolically the color of sky and ocean. The psychological associations are of contentment, gratification, and being at peace.

Green Often associated with the desire for better health, a useful life, or social reform, a person who possesses – or wishes to possess – high levels of self-esteem responds strongly to green.

Red This color's associations are with vitality, activity, desire, appetite and craving. The person who favors red is looking for intense experiences and to live a full life.

Yellow Primarily the color of happiness, lack of inhibition, cheerfulness, and expansiveness, people who favor yellow may be very productive, but that productivity often occurs sporadically.

Violet Representing a longing for wishes to be fulfilled and a desire to charm others, a preference for violet can communicate vulnerability or insecurity, perhaps a need for approval.

Brown Symbolic of "roots," hearth, home, and family security, a preference for brown suggests an increased need for physical ease and sensuous contentment, and for release from discomfort.

Black As the absolute boundary beyond which life ceases, it expresses the idea of nothingness, of extinction. Often seen as negative, it can enforce the characteristics of a color it surrounds.

What effect can color have on me?

Individuals often have emotional or physical symptoms, which can be alleviated and calmed by the use of certain colors. You may find yourself drawn to a color for one of two reasons. It may be your personality color, the shade that reflects you and best describes your beliefs, attitudes, and intellectual makeup. This color will help maintain your inner strengths and nourish you. Or it may be the color you need to redress an imbalance in your life – a color your body intuitively knows will help in a healing process.

Because of its positive effects on your personality and health, you'll want to incorporate your color into your life in many ways. Here are some ideas:

• Decorate your bedroom or study in a shade of your color, anything from the walls, to just a cushion cover. Bear in mind that a strong color, while powerful, can be overwhelming, but a more pastel version can be equally effective.

• Wear an item of clothing in your color or carry an accessory.

• Buy a mouse mat, mug, or desk accessory in your color, so that you have a permanent color fix while you're working. Glancing at your color throughout the day will keep you energized.

• Create a floral arrangement for your home, choosing flowers that epitomize your shade, such as red roses, yellow daffodils, or orange zinnias.

DO YOU FEEL SECURE?

Did you use a comforter as a child, or have a security blanket? Whilst the use of comforters is common in childhood, if your attachment to it was unusual, it may be a sign that you felt a need for more security and were apprehensive about something or life in general. We all need security, it's just that some of us seem to have it built-in, and others seek it from other sources.

Insecure people go through stages of self-doubt, and they tend to worry about things and to feel anxious. These feelings may be in response to current life events (such as moving house, or a relationship breakup) or they

TEST

Read through these questions, and answer each with a 'yes' or 'no' response:

Do you:

1. Express your views confidently in public?

2. Tend to stay calm in emotional situations?

3. Get annoyed with people who worry about the slightest thing?

4. Sometimes find it difficult to admit you are wrong?

5. Have absolute faith in yourself?

6. Trust your partner to be faithful?

7. Feel confident most of the time?

8. Find it hard to take criticism?

9. Enjoy performing in front of an audience?

10. Look forward rather than dwell over past experience?

may be characteristic (and as such just part of the psyche). While worrying can help the person anticipate dangers, be sensitive to others' reactions, and anticipate consequences of actions, it can also be painful and make a poor social impression on others.

Maybe you were the kind of child that never used a soother or cherished one teddy in particular. Secure people are self-assured, unworried and complacent. They tend to be self-confident and untroubled by self-doubt. While this may make them more resilient in stressful situations, at the extreme, the person's confidence may be unshakeable, even in situations that call for self-evaluation and self-improvement. Part of maturing is the ability to assess oneself and judge self-performance accurately. Secure people may not put themselves through this process because their belief in themselves is so strong.

SCORING/INTERPRETATION

If you answered yes to 7 or more questions – you are secure. You see yourself as self-sufficient, and look within yourself for strength, rather then turning to an outsider.

If you answered yes to 3 or less questions – you are insecure. You are more likely look to others for reassurance and support.

If you answered yes to between 4 and 6 questions – you are moderately secure.

If you are an insecure person, you will tend to have less confidence and belief in yourself, and look for reassurance from other sources, such as your partner, family or friends. As a result, you will receive a considerable amount of feedback, so make sure it is honest and not just given to placate you. However, these plentiful responses afford you the opportunity for strong personal growth – the first stage in developing as a person is in learning how others view you, and you are well along the right track.

If you are a secure person, you are probably confident and strong-willed, unlikely to be persuaded by peer pressure or swayed by group dynamics. You know your own mind and have the faith to stick to it. Your danger zone is that you may appear overly-confident and arrogant to others, who find your self-belief difficult to appreciate. Try to invite criticism or a critique of your abilities to ensure that you don't avoid hearing or learning anything negative about yourself.

If you are moderately secure, you will be a mostly confident person who has a few insecurities. These most commonly manifest themselves in personal appearance (most of us are insecure about how we look!), certain environments (such as starting a new job, or when arriving in a foreign country), or in interactions with particular people (talking to a senior manager at work, or being interviewed by the police). These insecurities are quite natural, just be aware of them and learn from them, drawing on your confident side to give yourself a little boost.

ARE YOU FLEXIBLE?

Flexibility is concerned with mental openness to new ideas, free thinking, and experimentation. The development of the modern Western world is built on this personality trait, as groups of intellectuals, artists, and scientists changed the world in some way through questioning, challenging, and innovating: from the artists and designers of Renaissance Italy, to the inventors and engineers of the Industrial Revolution in Britain, to the peace movement in San Francisco in the 1970s.

Flexible types tend to be open-minded and innovative, constantly looking for ways to change and improve the status quo. They tend to think critically and question authority, and if they're told that something's "always

TEST YOUR FLEXIBILITY

Have a look at these three different knots used for men's ties.

Would you stick to the four-in-hand, or try out new and different ways of presenting yourself? Would you consider a Windsor knot for certain occasions, or wear it whenever you felt like it?

The Four-in-Hand Knot – this is the standard tie knot, used throughout the world. It is the usual way of tying a tie, and is used for standard shirt collars.

The Half-Windsor Knot – this knot is slightly larger than a four-in-hand knot, but can still be used in standard shirt collars.

been done that way," it's like a red rag to a bull! They positively enjoy change, and get bored with routine. This can get frustrating for others, who find change for change's sake unsettling and frustrating.

Those particularly resistant to change are traditional types, who find comfort in the familiar. They tend to stick with the usual way of doing things and believe that "if it ain't broke, don't fix it." They prefer the predictable and a routine, so they don't tend to challenge the status quo. They are happy continuing with the way things are, reserving their energies for other issues. This can be annoying for change-seekers, and two people with personalities on the extreme ends of this trait will undoubtedly clash.

The Windsor Knot – this results in a particularly large knot, used in wide spread shirt collars. Attention is drawn to the tie because it is more prominent on the shirt.

SCORING/INTERPRETATION

If you like the Windsor and Half-Windsor knots and could imagine putting them into action straight away, you are likely to be flexible.

If you prefer the standard four-in-hand knot and would rather stick to what you know, you are likely to be traditional.

If you can see yourself trying the other knots occasionally, you are adaptable.

If you are flexible, you may love moving to a new apartment or house, just to try a new neighborhood, and renovating it once you get there. Perhaps you swap your car for a new model frequently, or love the latest fashions or music. Your danger zone will be in your relationships – continually seeking change may result in "itchy feet" at the thought of settling down.

If you are traditional, you will love to be surrounded by home comforts, and find habit soothing. You'll have a regular route to work, a set time to eat supper, and clothes to wear for certain occasions. This leaves you time and energy to pursue other interests, but you can become complacent in a situation, which could impact negatively on your happiness or career.

If you are adaptable, you are open to some change if you feel the timing and the situation is right. You could be persuaded to become more flexible or traditional, and would be a great partner for someone of either extreme, because you'd be able to accommodate him/her.

ARE YOU A PACK ANIMAL?

The Lone Ranger, a popular radio and TV western, was based on the exploits and adventures of John Reid, the sole survivor of an ambush. The masked man with the silver bullet was portrayed as a protector of the innocent, with an unswerving sense of justice, and a solitary *modus operandi.* In personality terms, he was a loner, enjoying time spent in his own company.

Since "loner" has negative connotations, "aloner" is a better term for the Lone Ranger, as he often worked with his partner, Tonto. Aloners are self-reliant, individualistic, and solitary. They rely on their own judgment, and may not discuss options with others, preferring to take the responsibility (and credit). They need their own personal space and time to recharge their batteries. This trait is important for any job in which there is autonomy and little interaction with colleagues (such as a traveling salesperson). The downside is that aloners find it difficult to operate collaboratively, an important skill in today's job market.

Group-oriented people, however, get a buzz from the energy that comes from people being together, so enjoy social clubs, working parties, even communal dinners. They make good team members, and thrive when "pulling together" is required, such as a care team or a theater company. Their downside is that they may lack the confidence to operate independently, and try to seek group approval before taking any decision.

TEST YOUR LIKING FOR WOLF, CHEETAH, OR LEOPARD

Wild animals live in a variety of social structures.

Wolves have a very sophisticated social organization, with a strict "pecking order" of dominance and supremacy. The top-ranking pair is known as the alpha male and alpha female, and this is normally the only pair that breeds. Wolves communicate with each other using facial expressions, gestures, and vocalizations, all of which reinforce the structure and cohesion of the pack. Wolf packs are usually between 4–8 in number.

Cheetahs have a unique and highly flexible social structure compared to other cats. Females tend to live alone (unless accompanied by cubs). The adults avoid each other but may share overlapping ranges. Most males also live alone, but some live in lifelong coalitions of 2–4 members. Males in coalitions tend to defend territories, whereas solitary males lead a more nomadic lifestyle.

If you are group-orientated, your life will be filled with friends, family, colleagues, and neighbors. You are great at networking, enjoy committees and fund-raising groups, and probably volunteer for project teams, relishing the opportunity to meet new people. However, there may be occasions when others look to you for direction or advice, and you may find it difficult to be decisive. Try to raise your comfort level for taking decisions by starting with something small – the time you take a lunch break or where you want to go at the weekend.

If you are affable, you are able both to enjoy teamwork and time spent on your own. The periods when you are alone will recharge your batteries for being in the company of others; likewise the occasions when you are with others energize you. Learn to enjoy both aspects of this trait. Taking pleasure in company and in solitude is a gift.

If you are an aloner, you are self-reliant and autonomous, and relatively introverted. You don't need the company of others to buoy you up; in fact, if you spend too long in the company of others, particularly people you don't know well, you start to plan your getaway. To keep from losing the art of conversation, and to develop interests that bring you into contact with like-minded enthusiasts, try to spend at least part of the day with other people.

Leopards are one of the prize sightings on a safari – stealthy and elusive. They are also surprisingly well camouflaged. Leopards lead a completely solitary lifestyle. Males inhabit territories of 2–15 square miles, which may overlap with the territories of several females. They are very defensive of their territory and urinate around the boundaries to warn off intruders.

Which animal do you identify with?

SCORING/INTERPRETATION

If you chose wolves, you are group-orientated.
If you chose cheetahs, you are affable.
If you chose leopards, you are an aloner.

ARE YOU A FREE SPIRIT?

Do you love the freedom and adventure of a trip where you just turn up at the airport with the plane tickets, not knowing where you'll stay when you arrive, or does that sound like a nightmare? Do you prefer a well-planned itinerary to make the most of your time, or is that your idea of organizational hell? The differences in these two approaches epitomize the poles of the perfectionism trait.

People who enjoy spontaneity are casual and comfortable leaving things to chance. They enjoy unpredictability and are flexible and don't worry about practicalities that much. They are good at jobs that involve dealing with chaotic or changeable information, such as air-traffic control, or police work. Those at the extreme end of this trait have to watch that they don't become disorganized, unprepared, or undisciplined.

Self-disciplined people tend to be perfectionists, goal-oriented, and exacting. They enjoy being organized, plan ahead, persevere, and work diligently. They excel at jobs in human resources or logistics, where their organizational skills are valued. They feel uncomfortable in unstructured or chaotic situations, and may try to impose a plan or create order. Sometimes this is needed, such as when looking after small children; other times this is frustrating and annoying for others, particularly in casual social situations.

TEST YOUR ELEMENTARY NATURE

Consider the four elements of life: fire, water, air, and earth. These are often linked to the four humors, as described by Hippocrates, or to the zodiacal signs. For the purposes of this exercise, try to think of the elements in a different way: How spontaneous are they? How controllable? How predictable? Which element's personality do you see in yourself?

If you are a spontaneous person, you are great fun as a friend, and encourage others to forget their hassles and live life to the full. However, you can be unexacting and sloppy. While this doesn't matter when you're on your own, when you are with others, it may irritate them, and make them see you as inefficient or lazy – even though you aren't. Try to tune into other people's perceptions of you.

If you are self-disciplined, you are most effective in organized and structured situations. You like predictability and work to a routine that maximizes your time. However, you find it hard to deal with unpredictability, and can seem inflexible and dogmatic. You need to judge which situations really matter, and which can be let go.

If you are flexible, you may be able to "switch on" spontaneity or self-discipline, depending on the situation. If so, you'll fit in to most groups and become known for your efficiency at work, because you don't sweat the small stuff. But maybe you don't switch from one side to another, and are genuinely in between – a little bit organized, enjoying some spontaneity. Practice swapping your behavior between one extreme and the other.

SCORING/INTERPRETATION

Fire is unpredictable and often very difficult to control. If you chose fire, you are spontaneous.

Earth is generally steadfast and slow to change. If you chose earth, you are self-disciplined.

Air and water can be controlled and contained to a certain degree, although they retain some unpredictability. If you chose either of these, you are flexible.

DO YOU LIKE THE BUZZ OR THE ZZZZS?

What sort of vacations do you take? For most people, a holiday is an opportunity to escape from work or domestic duties, and to experience a new environment. Urban dwellers may seek the calm and relaxing countryside; suburbanites may enjoy a city break or a busy beach resort. The need for tranquility and peace, or an energy buzz from being around people, applies to our personalities as well as the environments we seek out.

Tranquil people are relaxed and placid. They are like a cool stream meandering gently through a meadow. They are not easily upset or aroused, and frustrations rarely bother them. They are good at jobs where patience and a cool head are required, such as teaching or nursing. The downside of a laidback approach to life is that tranquil people can find it hard to get motivated, and they can appear disinterested and lethargic to others.

Tense people are driven and have high energy levels. They are like 42nd Street on a Saturday night. Tense people can be impatient and irritable, but there are benefits to this "tension" – a certain amount is often necessary to focus effectively. Tense personalities are motivated and action-orientated, and are also great at motivating others.

If you are a tranquil individual, you are laidback, easy-going, and composed. Your relaxed personality style rubs off on other people, who find you a calm and stress-free friend or partner. However, your wide comfort zone, and your lower energy and arousal levels mean you may be disinclined to change or push yourself. Do you have any unfulfilled ambitions, however small? Make a plan for making some a reality.

If you are tense, you are energized, action-orientated, and a "doer." You probably drive yourself hard to improve and play well. Your energy is infectious, and you have the charisma to change things for the better. However, you are prone to being highly-strung and nervy. You must learn to relax, so that you don't burn out. Try listening to a relaxation tape or music that you love – practice doing nothing!

If you are composed, you are probably inclined toward either a tranquil or a tense style, but have learned techniques to pull yourself back from an extreme. This is a good way of managing your personality. Consider which type – tranquil or tense – you feel is the most like you. Can you switch back to your natural style if you need to?

TEST YOUR ATTITUDE TOWARD WINNING

In Aesop's fable, a tortoise and a hare had an argument about who was faster. They decided to settle the argument with a race. They agreed on a route and set off. The hare shot ahead and was soon in the lead by some distance. Seeing that he was a long way ahead of the tortoise, the hare thought he'd take a break and relax for a while. He sat under a tree and soon fell asleep. Meanwhile, the tortoise plodded on and overtook him, and soon finished the race, emerging as the undisputed winner. The hare woke up just in time to see the turtle pass the finishing line.

The hare seemed poised to win, but he was rather arrogant and became distracted. The tortoise plodded steadily on, but he was lucky to win the race. Are you more like the hare or the tortoise?

SCORING/INTERPRETATION

If you are more like the tortoise, you are a tranquil person.

If you are more like the hare, you are a tense person.

If you can see elements of yourself in both characters, you are composed.

YOUR INTERNAL TRAITS PROFILE

If you've completed every internal trait test, you can profile your results to get an overall view of your "internal" personality, how you really are inside. Circle the relevant boxes for each of your test scores, then add up the circled items you have in each column.

	A	B	C	SCORING
Pages 26–27	Warm	Lukewarm	Cool	**If you have the most circled items** in Column A, you are emotionally dependent.
Pages 28–29	Creative	Center-brained	Logical	
Pages 30–31	Emotionally reactive	Emotionally balanced	Emotionally stable	
Pages 32–33	Deferential	Assertive	Dominant	
Pages 34–35	Lively	Equable	Serious	**If you have the most circled items** in Column B or an equal number in any two columns, you are emotionally neutral.
Pages 36–37	Rule-breaker	Rule-chooser	Rule-conscious	
Pages 38–39	Socially bold	Socially cautious	Socially shy	
Pages 42–43	Sensitive	Sense-aware	Unsentimental	
Pages 44–45	Trusting	Tentative	Vigilant	
Pages 46–47	Heaven-bound	Horizon-bound	Earth-bound	
Pages 48–49	Open	Tactful	Discreet	**If you have the most circled items** in Column C you are emotionally self-sufficient.
Pages 52–53	Insecure	Moderately secure	Secure	
Pages 54–55	Flexible	Adaptable	Traditional	
Pages 56–57	Group-orientated	Affable	Aloner	
Pages 58–59	Spontaneous	Flexible	Self-disciplined	
Pages 60–61	Tranquil	Composed	Tense	
Total number				

INTERPRETATION

Emotionally dependent

You are one of those people who need the emotional closeness of relationships. You don't take things too seriously, and have a relaxed approach to life. You form strong and stable bonds with colleagues, friends, and partners and are good at anticipating other people's feelings. You try to see the good in other people. You look beyond the here and now, are spiritually aware, and in touch with nature and the world outside.

However, you can also be insecure, and your emotions are pretty well always on show and rarely in check, which can be overwhelming for other people. You like things to be pleasant at all cost, cringe at confrontation, and will defer to stronger characters rather than fight your corner. You don't like hurting people's feelings, which can lead to indecision and frustration for everyone involved.

Emotionally self-sufficient

You like order, predictability, and rules. You have routines that you stick to, and are a stickler for deadlines and arriving places on time. You enjoy your own company and can wile away the hours alone on hobbies and pastimes. You are cool, calm and collected, in control of your emotions and your life. You seldom lose your temper.

And the drawbacks? Well, you are essentially inward-focused, and have a tendency to dwell too much on your own perspective on life and events. Your lack of emotional warmth can be interpreted as distance, reserve, and mistrust. Your need for order and predictability means that you can come across as inflexible and dogmatic. To live a little and loosen up would be good advice!

Emotionally neutral

You probably combine the best and worst qualities of being relationship dependent and emotionally self-sufficient. The plus side is that you achieve a good balance between emotional warmth and distance in appropriate situations. You aren't too emotionally needy, but neither are you aloof or detached. You enjoy a little spontaneity as long as you have some order in your life.

However, you may have the ability to be mainly relationship dependent or emotionally self-sufficient depending on the situation, and this might be conscious or subconscious. Ask yourself whether you seem to switch personality types – it's quite common to behave differently at home than you do at work, for example, or differently with your friends than you do with your parents.

PART 2

EXTERNAL TRAITS

WHAT ARE EXTERNAL TRAITS?

Personality can be categorized and measured in many different ways – there are nearly as many theories as there are psychologists! A popular way of breaking down personality into measurable chunks, is into "traits," individual features that are possessed to a greater or lesser degree. We do this ourselves when we say that someone is "caring," "outspoken," or "confident." On a scale from "very outspoken" to "very quiet," we can pretty easily categorize everyone we know (including ourselves), although psychologists would look for more proof than just an opinion! The important thing to remember is that traits are possessed in varying quantities, part of what makes personality a kaleidoscope of permutations and possibilities. Every person is different.

The elements of personality that influence interactions with other people are of great interest to organizations in selecting, recruiting, and developing staff. The vast majority of jobs need specific people skills; for example, some positions involve contact with customers and people for these jobs are usually recruited with particular care because they will represent the organization to the outside world. Other jobs may center around working with computers, having fewer opportunities for social interaction, and would suit a quiet person rather than a gregarious one.

An important aspect of personality testing is that employers usually have a good idea of the personality profile that would match a job specification. If you don't get a job or promotion, you may have been done a favor in the long run if the day-to-day interactions of the job clash with your personality style.

Some of the most well-known personality tests in the world are based on external traits, or include measurement of them in the questionnaire. One of these is the OPQ® questionnaire, developed by the psychometric test publishers SHL in direct response for a need for a personality test focused on work contexts.

The OPQ® evaluates 32 traits, divided in three categories, one of which is "Relationships with People." The test-takers rate themselves from 1 to 5 on a variety of statements, such as "I enjoy talking to new people." Each trait has several statements linked to it, so that as you complete the questionnaire, an overall picture emerges of your profile.

This chapter contains tests that measure your external traits, those relevant to how you react to external events and individuals, how you interact and behave when other people are around. Make sure you read through the test instructions carefully, but don't spend too long thinking of an answer or the correct response – the first thing that comes into your mind is usually the most accurate reflection of how you are.

You may want to consider whether you are taking the test for self-knowledge or as preparation for a job. Many people think and behave differently at home than they do at work; generally, a person's "at home" persona is his or her true self, and the person's "work" persona reflects how he or she would like others to see him or her. You might be a very forward person at work, respectful of hierarchies, and keen to ensure your successes are noticed, but a modest person in your private life, disinterested in status, and reluctant to talk about yourself.

Exploring your external traits will help you understand more about how you relate to others, and your communication with colleagues, friends, family, peers, and partners. Are you a people person?

Please note: This chapter contains simplified personality tests based on personality trait theory. It is not a replacement for the full OPQ® questionnaire or any other professional personality test, and the results are not intended to be the psychometric or practical equivalent to OPQ® questionnaire results.

ARE YOU GOOD AT SPEAKING UP?

Think of an orchestra, with its many instruments. These instruments work together to produce a harmonious sound. Some take center stage, such as a solo instrument in a concerto, or the lead violin, which tends to play the melody in a piece. Others, such as the double bass or percussion instruments, have vital but supporting roles. Their notes enhance and enrich the music, but are generally in the background.

All of us have traits reflecting the emotional and behavioral preferences we are born with, although some people work hard to shift or mask their personalities.

TEST YOUR OUTSPOKENNESS

Imagine this scene, or act it out in a role-play on your own.

You're having a meal with friends in a neighborhood restaurant, and the food just isn't up to scratch – the portions are small, the cooking poor, and dishes arrived at different times. You all have a bit of a moan, and laugh about it. What, if anything, would you actually do?

Pick the response that best fits your natural personality:
(a) Call the waiter over to complain on behalf of the group; you don't want a bad meal to ruin the evening.
(b) Say "yes" when the waiter comes to ask you if everything is OK – you don't want to spoil the atmosphere for everyone.
(c) When the waiter comes to ask if everything is OK, say that it wasn't great but that you'll eat it.

One trait that people commonly seek to acquire, if they haven't been born with it, is outspokenness. This is because a life permanently in the shadows can be unfulfilling. Just as there have been solo pieces written for percussion, extreme social timidity can be overcome. Outspoken people express their opinions quite freely because they believe in their right to do so. They don't feel uncomfortable about disagreements with other people and are prepared to criticize others if the criticism is justified. The essence of their approach to interactions is that nothing is personal. They can seem brash, tactless, and too direct to others.

Quiet people don't, as a rule, speak up. They tend to find it difficult to say "no" or to complain because they are anxious about another person's feelings or reactions, and they don't want to draw attention to themselves.

There are even some workplaces where disagreement and outspokenness is definitely frowned upon; in the armed forces, for example, talking back is a disciplinary offence.

However, people who bottle up things may erupt in a sudden explosion of anger as the original thought or feeling usually persists.

SCORING/INTERPRETATION

If you chose (a) – you are an outspoken type.

If you chose (b) – you are a quiet type.

If you chose (c) – you are prudent.

If you are an outspoken type, you'll speak your mind, and expect others to do the same. You enjoy verbal banter, and see disagreements as a healthy and straightforward expression of views – nothing more. The plus side of being outspoken is that you are unlikely to be exploited by colleagues or downtrodden by your partner. The minus side is that you may upset people with your forthright talk. Outspokenness has a tendency to tip into aggression, or perceived aggression anyway, so be aware of other people's rights and feelings, even if they don't speak up about them.

If you are a quiet type, you'll keep your opinions to yourself, unless asked, and even then you are careful about how you express them. You are a discreet friend and colleague, and are probably trusted with sensitive information or gossip. However, your weakness is that you find it hard to say "no." Most quiet people have conversations in their heads about how to resolve a conflict they're in; but still, their mouths say "yes," while their heads say "no." Use charm, humor, or even deliberate manipulation to get you what you want without having to attempt behavior that may go against your personality.

If you are prudent, you'll know where you are along the outspoken-quiet continuum. At the quiet end, are those who do speak up for themselves, but without much force. At the outspoken end are the more assertive types, who are good at standing up for themselves, but who still consider other people's feelings and motivations. In general, assertive approaches to a situation achieve the best all-around and lasting solutions.

CAN YOU CHANGE OTHERS' OPINIONS?

All major companies employ public relations (or PR) professionals to present corporate news in the most favorable light. Political parties appoint "spin doctors" to control how policy is conveyed to the public, and even to discredit the opposition in the eyes of the electorate. It is widely accepted that the media, particularly TV and the newspapers, can win or lose elections for individuals or parties. Power and commercial success are ultimately decided by the general public, so organizations have developed expertise in trying to change our opinions.

On a smaller scale, changing opinion can be about selling – a product, a service, a course of action, or even yourself. Persuasive people enjoy selling and changing other people's opinions. They are good at negotiating, putting forward convincing arguments, and trying to present things to the best advantage. They enjoy influencing the outcome of discussions and persuading others to their points of view. They will certainly use this skill either in a job or in the local community. If you've ever found yourself drafted in to help with something, a persuasive person was the reason!

Uninfluential types don't enjoy selling or persuading others to their points of view – they are quite happy with their own opinions and perspectives and don't feel the need to change other people's opinions. They find it harder to influence the outcome of discussions and tend not to want to get involved in situations requiring diplomacy. They are straightforward and direct people, who would rather say what they think and what they want, than use "devious" means.

TEST YOUR PERSUASIVENESS

The classic board game Monopoly was created by Charles Darrow during the Great Depression. For place names, he named the squares on the boards after his favorite seaside resort, Atlantic City. He handcrafted the houses and hotels in wood, hand-wrote the title deeds and cards, and for the playing pieces, used charms from his wife's bracelet. Parkers Brothers bought the game in 1935, and in its first year Monopoly became the best-selling game in America.

As with all board games, Monopoly players tend to have their

If you are a persuasive type, you'll enjoy interacting with people in challenging situations, and will get a real buzz from a successful outcome in your favor. You are probably assertive, controlling, and socially confident, and not easily intimidated. You have a clear idea of what you want and where you are going. Your danger zone is that others, particularly uninfluential types, may not trust or believe in you or what you say. Make sure you tread gently, and adapt your style and approach as necessary.

If you are an uninfluential type, you tend to avoid confrontations and feel that your opinions are best kept to yourself unless someone invites you to express them. You are probably an introverted and quiet person. The down side is that you can come across as self-contained and fixed in your own ideas. You also may feel unfulfilled or undervalued due to your reluctance to engage in a dialogue that might result in a disagreement or unpleasantness. Practice negotiation by taking part in discussions that don't have an emotional undercurrent – you can then relax and enjoy the debate.

If you are plain-speaking and you chose (c) in the test, you'll pride yourself on your straightforwardness because you feel the best approach is to be honest and direct about what you want. Watch out that your plain-speaking approach doesn't offend those more sensitive than you. If you chose (d) in the test, you have basic negotiation skills that just need honing, or perhaps you need a little more confidence to take a discussion further. Build up your self-belief by setting yourself small targets you can succeed at.

favored playing piece – the top hat, the dog, the ship, the car, the iron or the boot – and may even consider it lucky. Imagine you are playing Monopoly with friends, and your absolute favorite playing piece is chosen by another player.

Which of the following would best reflect your actions?
(a) Would you negotiate a deal that enabled you to have the piece you wanted?
(b) Would you say nothing, and choose another?
(c) Would you ask him or her to let you have it?
(d) Would you attempt to persuade the other player to swap, but probably fail?

SCORING/INTERPRETATION

If you chose (a) – you are a persuasive type.
If you chose (b) – you are an uninfluential type.
If you chose (c) or (d) – you are plain-speaking.

DO YOU TAKE CHARGE?

There are certain situations that cry out for someone to take charge – a traffic accident, the scene of a crime, a group expedition – situations where a degree of control must be exerted to maintain security or safety. There are situations in everyday life, too, where we need to take charge of our own lives – moving home, changing jobs, or raising kids.

Controlling types positively enjoy taking charge, and look for areas outside of their private lives where they can contribute and do this. They like to make decisions for a group, put suggestions forward, volunteer for tasks, and enjoy giving instructions to others. As a result of their "I'm in charge" aura, others look to them when solutions need to be found. They make natural leaders, and excel in management and team leadership roles.

Compliant types contribute less to group activities and are reluctant to put forward suggestions when

TEST YOUR COMPLIANCY

The Orkneys are a group of small, remote islands in northern Scotland. A well-known Orcadian folk story is called "The Sea Mither" (mother).

The Sea Mither represented the benign force of the summer sea, granting life, bringing warmth to the oceans, and calming Orkney storms. She had a very powerful and hostile rival in Teran, the spirit of winter. Each spring, the Sea Mither and Teran battled for control of the sea, resulting in storms and rough seas. The Sea Mither always triumphed in this battle and her benign reign returned, calming the seas. But as winter approached, Teran would become stronger and break free, and the Sea Mither, exhausted by her work over the summer, was banished. Teran reigned supreme over the winter months, subjecting all living creatures to his evil and tyrannous rule. But when spring arrived, the Sea Mither would decisions need to be made. They dislike taking a lead in groups, and would never volunteer for this role, which actually makes them feel quite uncomfortable. They prefer not to structure the work of other people, and tend to look to others when decisions need to be made. They can make great team members because they will support the team leader wholeheartedly.

SCORING/INTERPRETATION

If you are like the Sea Mither and Teran, you are a controlling type.

If you are like the sea, you are a compliant type.

If you can see yourself as controller and controlled, you are reasonable.

---

prepare herself for battle again, and refreshed and invincible, she would emerge victorious in the summer.

These two forces, the Sea Mither and Teran, are personifications of the good and bad sides of a desire to control. Do you see elements of yourself in this? Or perhaps you are more like the sea, the subject of the control, searching for a leader.

If you are a controlling type, you will thrive on directing, managing, and organizing others. Perhaps you are the one who instigates regular family get-togethers or gets involved with school and neighborhood events or fund-raising, or you might apply for a job that involves controlling the work of teams. The Sea Mither demonstrates the beneficial aspects of controlling others, whereas Teran shows how a controlling influence can be destructive and despised and hated by those the controller is trying to manage. "Teran" behavior is your danger zone.

If you are a compliant type, you don't like taking the lead or having to dictate to others. If you tend toward extravertism, you will enjoy working with people but enjoy the camaraderie of a team too much to manage it. If you tend toward introvertism, you are probably regarded as a quiet and reserved person, who is agreeable and acquiescent. In either case, you should not feel pressurized into a more high-powered role, or to take on tasks you feel uncomfortable with; on the other hand, just check with yourself that you are happy with a low level of influence.

If you are reasonable, there is probably some dichotomy in your approach to control. Perhaps you seek control at home or at work, but not both arenas. Perhaps you exert control within your team at work, but readily comply with more senior managers. The important issue is that your talent for control is used somehow, because you will feel frustrated if it has no outlet.

DO YOU HAVE STRONG VIEWS?

Freedom of expression is a central concept of democracy. The public criticism of government, which, after all, is elected by the people for the people, results in an essential reality check on policies. Free speech also allows citizens to raise issues that have been forgotten or ignored by government or the public; there are many examples of pressure groups raising public consciousness on an issue and succeeding in changing policy or law.

Independent people speak up even if their views are unpopular, and make it plain when they disagree with a group. They are prepared to go it alone if others disagree, and have the strength of character not to care what others think – if they believe something is wrong, they feel they must speak out, regardless of any consequences. They enjoy acting on their own, and can feel suffocated by too many ties or constraints on their actions. They excel at jobs that allow them the freedom to determine their own work such as self-employment of any kind, investigative journalism, or political lobbying.

Reliant types are at the opposite end of the spectrum. They are less

TEST YOUR DEGREE OF INDEPENDENCE

Gemstones have traditionally been valued not just for their physical beauty but also for particular emotional attributes and personality traits with which they are associated. Look at the pictures of each stone. Which gemstone are you most attracted to?

CARNELIAN

PERIDOT

ROSE QUARTZ

inclined to do their own thing, and would rather be part of a group. They tend to go along with what the group decides even though they may have different opinions themselves. Their views are not held so strongly, and they will hold back from expressing an opinion if they feel it might create a bad atmosphere. This apparent easy-goingness means they are very manageable as employees or committee members. You are unlikely to get an honest opinion, though, if it differs from your own!

SCORING/INTERPRETATION

Carnelian is associated with confidence and energy, repels negativity, and encourages you to awaken hidden talents, fulfil your dreams, speak up for yourself, and get out into the world. If you identified with carnelian, you are an independent type.

Peridot is associated with solving problems and healing the mind, helping you to understand things or behaviors that might be holding you back. This stone appeals to people who would benefit from some reassurance when standing up for themselves – nurturing their own needs and expressing themselves on their terms, so if peridot was your stone of choice, you are judicious.

Rose Quartz is a powerful love stone, associated with personal attraction and relationships, drawing together groups of friends who protect each other from loneliness and provide love and mutual support. If you identified with rose quartz, you are reliant.

If you are an independent type, you'll have strong opinions on things and are likely to stand up for yourself, your rights, and your beliefs. You like to feel free to do what you want, enjoy pursuing your own interests, making your own rules, and are self- or individually-orientated. You like being in control and are confident, and don't worry too much about what other people think about you. However, you can ride roughshod over other people in pursuit of your own ideals, so watch other people's reactions to your comments very carefully for signs of discomfort or emotional upset.

If you are a reliant type, you value social interaction and security, are reluctant to rock the boat, and put others ahead of your own needs or wishes. You are happy working within constraints and rules, and, in fact, find it quite comforting to know where you stand. You have a democratic approach to managing your job and your life, and believe that there are times when the best thing to say is nothing. Your danger zone is that you may regret not speaking out about something, for moral or personal reasons, so make sure your silence is based on tactics rather than lack of confidence.

If you are judicious, you probably feel fairly comfortable with expressing your views, and use your judgment to determine when to speak and when to stay mute. Take a moment to assess some recent situations where you either spoke out or you chose not to. Did you act wisely? Would you behave the same way if you had your time again?

ARE YOU FUN-LOVING?

Do you know someone who loves jokes, playing tricks on people, and being the life of the party? If so, he or she is a full-on gregarious type. These people are outgoing, vibrant, and happy-go-lucky. They tend to live for the moment and enjoy entertaining and cheering people up, and believe in being jovial. Gregarious people are great company, although their approach to life can feel superficial – everything's a joke with them, very little is sacred or "off-limits" in terms of a target for their wit. It can wear thin if you aren't in the mood for laughing, or you may find their comments tactless or offensive.

At the other end of the scale are the serious folk among us. They are more inhibited and reserved. They feel uncomfortable when in the limelight and are less spontaneous and talkative. They treat people and events seriously, and they feel that joking about things downgrades their importance.

LEPRECHAUN, GNOME, OR ELF?

All countries and cultures have a history of storytelling that includes mythical creatures – living beings that are neither human nor a known animal species. These creatures tend to have personality traits assigned to them. They are often troublesome or outright dangerous, as myths were used as a way of communicating values and desirable behaviors to children; others are benign, or just mischievous.

The leprechaun, for example, is of Celtic origin, a small fairy known for being a shoemaker. It is usually depicted dressed in green with a leather apron and silver buckled shoes. The mythology of gnomes originates in Europe, where these woodland creatures gather their food, and live underground or in trees. The stories of elves come from northern Europe, such as Santa's elves in Lapland who help him organize Christmas.

Which are you? A leprechaun, gnome, or an elf?

A downside is that such people can be perceived as a bit dull and boring – the "mask" rarely slips, even in less formal situations such as a company party. They become embarrassed easily and rarely let their hair down. This makes them more difficult to get to know, although their friendship, once gained, can be rewarding and enjoyable.

SCORING/INTERPRETATION

Leprechauns love playing tricks, and are known for their fun-loving and mischievous natures. If you catch a leprechaun, which is difficult, he must reveal the location of his hidden treasure. But if you take your eye off him for even a second, he will disappear. If you are like fun-loving and mischievous leprechauns, you are a gregarious type.

Gnomes live a very long time, about 250 years, and are known for their quiet wisdom. They avoid conflict if at all possible, because they are gentle and peaceful creatures, and help resolve the disagreements of other groups. They are most happy at home, dozing by the fire. If you are like gentle and retiring gnomes, you are a serious type.

Elves are generally known to be patient, calm, and peaceful in nature, and unlike other mythical creatures they work with and assist humans willingly. They respect all living things and are brought up to respect and be at one with nature. They can also be playful and enjoy life and have a cheeky side to them. If you are like the elves, you are amiable.

If you are a gregarious type, you have a gift for raising people's spirits and cheering them up, and are great fun to be around. Your enthusiasm for life is infectious, and you would do well working in the entertainment industry, or in sales, as you can get along with people and they feel good around you. You need, however, to be careful of misjudging situations by injecting a note of fun which isn't appreciated or appropriate. When speaking with others, look for clues to the person's mood, and see if you can "swallow" a flippant remark instead of blurting it out.

If you are more serious, you'll prefer to spend time getting to know people before you make a joke or tease them. You may love parties and social occasions, but more as a spectator than an active participant. You would thrive in jobs where joking around would be frowned upon, such as the caring professions. However, you need to relax around other people if they're to feel you like them and want to be with them, crucial for forming new friendships. Make sure you smile, relax your body language, and join in conversations at social events – that way you'll give out friendly vibes.

If you are amiable, you probably tend toward one end of the spectrum. Perhaps you are really a serious type, but have urged yourself to lighten up and join in more. Or, you may be naturally gregarious, but tone it down when you're not feeling especially effervescent. Adjusting your gregariousness depending on the current situation is a sophisticated social skill.

DO YOU ENJOY COMPANIONSHIP?

In the past, it was common for an aristocratic unmarried or widowed lady to have a "companion" – another woman paid to accompany her on her travels or outings, and to provide regular company and companionship. A lady's companion was usually an educated woman who was herself single, and needed to earn an income, but her role enjoyed high status.

Today, too, we place a high value on friendship, particularly as family members are often scattered. Friendship-focused folk are sociable, maintaining a wide circle of friends, and enjoy being in groups. They prefer to do things with other people, rather than on their own, and seek out company wherever possible. They share feelings, events, and details about their lives with friends, and tend to form strong attachments to people.

On the other hand, aloof people enjoy their own company, and tend to have a narrower range of friends,

TEST YOUR COMPANIONSHIP

The concept of companionship is echoed in nature. There is a wide variety of social behavior in birds – some species pair for life, others only meet to mate. Some birds live together in flocks, others live a solitary existence.

Look at these two birds. Do you feel they are alone or are they companions? Are they just watching each other, or are they interacting through body language or birdsong? If you were one of the birds, would you seek out the company of the other?

although these may be deep and secure relationships. They consider themselves loners and take pleasure from spending time alone, finding it a therapeutic way of recharging their batteries. They often have hobbies that can be pursued independently, and jobs which enable them to have time away from colleagues.

SCORING/INTERPRETATION

If you think the birds are companions, you are a sociable type.

If you feel they are temporarily sharing the same place, you are an aloof type.

If you have no strong feelings either way, you are an agreeable type.

If you are a sociable type, you'll love being with friends and having company. You will network like crazy, and build up a large number of friendships, whether at work or in your private life. You'll be the person who organizes reunions, family get-togethers, and social events, and you will relish being at the center of things. You would excel in a corporate environment, where networking can lead to new business or career advancement, or in a knowledge-based environment, where you can draw on a wide range of your specialist contacts. However, you may find it hard to be productive or motivated if you are on your own. Try going to the movies or a restaurant alone; take a book or some magazines, and see if you can enjoy the experience.

If you are aloof, you'll enjoy the peace and solitude of spending time on your own, suiting yourself. You find the idea of joining anything – a social club or society – makes you feel uncomfortable, unless the socializing aspect is minimal. You don't tend to keep in contact with old friends, although if someone else is organizing something, you might go along. You would do well in a job where you have the psychological and physical space to work on your own, and you don't have to rely too much on other people. You need, however, to ensure that your social skills don't get rusty through lack of regular contact and interaction with others. Try to set yourself a target to counter this; chat with someone at the water cooler once a day, or phone a friend you haven't seen in a while.

If you are agreeable, you probably balance the two needs in yourself – to be with other people so you don't get lonely, and to be on your own for some peace and quiet. You are good company and are sought out socially because you don't hog the limelight. Your challenge is to ensure that you do make time for yourself to be alone if you need it, and to push yourself center-stage when you feel particularly sociable.

ARE YOU AT EASE WITH STRANGERS?

There was a time when strangers were welcomed, as a source of interest or news, in a time where communications were slow and people traveled less and over shorter distances. Today, we rely on television and newspapers for news, and saying "hello" to everyone you pass is simply not viable.

Some people feel instinctively comfortable meeting new people, seeing it as an opportunity to learn something new and make a fresh acquaintance. These socially confident people are good at putting others at their ease, and find it easy to think of conversation topics to keep the interaction friendly and lively. They are confident with unfamiliar people. Have you ever been the recipient of help or kindness from a stranger? He or she was probably a socially confident person, comfortable with strangers.

There are often sound reasons to feel uncomfortable with strangers. You don't know if you can trust a stranger; you know nothing about the individual, or his or her values, or background. However, socially hesitant people hold back from all strangers, in every situation, even a "safe" one. They feel tense when meeting new people, becoming tongue-tied when talking to others. They feel uncomfortable unless they know people well, but with close friends and family, they are relaxed and good company.

TEST YOUR SOCIABILITY

You are at a friend's house for dinner, and the doorbell rings. Your friend answers the door and introduces you to a work colleague who is picking up some papers on the way home. Your friend excuses him- or herself to check on progress in the kitchen, leaving you alone with the colleague.

Would you feel this situation was (a) an opportunity to meet someone new or (b) uncomfortable?

Would you (a) speak first, or (b) wait to be spoken to?

Could you think of five topics of conversation? (a) yes (b) no

You could role-play this with a friend to test your responses.
1. How would you feel as your friend left?
(a) Panicky.
(b) Uncomfortable.
(c) Relaxed.

SCORING/INTERPRETATION

If you chose (c) responses you are a socially confident type.
If you chose (a) responses you are a socially hesitant type.
If you chose (b) responses you are a socially comfortable type.

2. What would you be thinking?
(a) "What a nightmare!"
(b) "I need to think of something to say!"
(c) I wouldn't be thinking anything – I'd just start chatting.

3. Could you keep a five-minute conversation going with this stranger?
(a) Definitely not.
(b) Probably.
(c) Yes, easily.

4. What would you do when your friend returned from the kitchen?
(a) Let him resume lead of the conversation.
(b) Excuse yourself politely, so that the two of them can talk about work.
(c) Explain the topic of conversation and encourage him to join in.

If you are socially confident, you are good with people and enjoy putting them at their ease and bringing out the best in them. You'll be a popular guest at parties or social events because you mix well. You would be great at any job that involved working with the public, such as journalism or retail. Your danger zone is that talking to strangers can be easier than talking to your close friends or your partner – there are no difficult emotional issues or "baggage" from previous encounters. Ensure that you aren't neglecting your close relationships or avoiding intimacy.

If you are socially hesitant, you probably find it hard to make conversation and feel uneasy in meetings or gatherings where you do not know people well. Your idea of a nightmare would be giving a speech or presentation in front of a room full of strangers – you would much rather spend time with familiar faces in a non-threatening atmosphere. You would enjoy a job where you work in a team, so that you can get to know people well. However, you may be cutting yourself off from new experiences and friendships, which limits your personal development opportunities. Try going to social events with a more confident friend, and join in established conversations – it's easier than starting them from scratch.

If you are socially comfortable, you may find some situations easier than others, or may feel socially confident one day, and shyer the next, depending on your mood. Many people switch on social confidence for work, but find it draining as it goes against their personalities. If this becomes too much pressure, consider changing jobs to something that reflects your natural traits better.

WHAT'S YOUR NUMBER?

You've probably heard of numerology, but what is it? Numerology is a tool for self-discovery, which traces its roots back many centuries. Pythagoras, the Greek mathematician who lived from 569-470 BC is said to be the father or originator of what is today called numerology.

Numerology is the study of numbers, and the manner in which they reflect certain aptitudes and character tendencies. The basic idea is that who we are is influenced to some extent by the numbers in our lives. These are drawn from our birth name (each letter has a numerical value which is summed), and the sum of numbers in our birth date. These numbers are believed to reveal a great deal about our character, purpose in life, motivations, and talents.

There are eleven numbers used in constructing numerology charts. These numbers are 1, 2, 3, 4, 5, 6, 7, 8, 9, 11, and 22. Each of these numbers represents different characteristics and expressions. Larger numbers that occur from adding the numbers in the complete birth date or from the values assigned to each name are reduced by adding the digits together until the sum achieved is one of the core numbers. Just add the components of the larger number together (repeatedly, if necessary) until a single digit results. For example, the year 1968 becomes 1+9+6+8 which equals 24, which in turn is separated into its digits, so 2+4 equals 6.

The "master numbers" 11 and 22 are the only exceptions to rule of reducing to a single digit; if the number 11 or 22 results from an addition, you stop at this point. Master numbers suggest a great potential for learning and achievement. They are intensified versions of the single digit number they replace (2 for 11 and 4 for 22).

Finding significant numbers

The starting point of numerology is often the date of birth. This date is used to determine what is called the "life path number," and this aspect of Numerology is easily grasped. Using the reduction principle described, you can find your life path number – and the qualities it is said to encompass.

Write down your birth date as mm/dd/yyyy. If you were born on August 10, 1982, for example, you would write 08/10/1982. The month becomes 0+8=8, the day 1+0=1, and the year 1+9+8+2=20, then 2+0 = 2. The next sum is to add these reductions, 8+1+2, which equals 11. Since 11 is a master number, you stop there. Now you have a try!

THE NUMBERS AND WHAT THEY MEAN

Each number corresponds to a range of personality factors, some favorable, some less so.

Independent, creative, competitive, hates being bored, achieving, boastful, arrogant.

Good at organizing and fact-finding, commonsensical, fair-minded, non-confrontational, weak.

Good at speaking out, excellent social skills, enthusiastic, charming, vain, materialistic.

Practical, dedicated, work-focused, good at problem-solving, demanding, egocentric.

Open-minded, inquisitive, eager to learn, adaptable, tolerant, lazy, seeks fast gratification.

Compassionate, empathetic, logical, artistic, caring, supportive, emotionally needy.

Organized, peaceful, idealistic, motivated, analytical, impatient, dislikes taking advice.

Strong, leadership qualities, responsible, respected, controlling, angers quickly.

Passionate, compassionate, socially responsible, enjoys learning, intellectual, tendency to "use" people.

Spiritual, knowledgeable, intuitive, cultured, visionary, tendency to mood swings, hard to motivate.

Talented, potential for success, achieving, charismatic, practical, dictatorial, insensitive.

How can I use numerology?

You can incorporate numerology and your life plan number into your life in many ways.

Calculate the life plan numbers for your partner, family members, and close friends. Share the results with them and talk about whether you feel the results reflect your personalities.

Remember your life plan number, and find ways of bringing it into your life. If your number is 7, for example, you might wear a ring with seven stones, fill a vase with seven roses, wear a jacket with seven buttons, or even live on the seventh floor!

Your life plan number reflects how you will approach things throughout your life. Write down examples of important actions or feelings and see if your reactions reflected your life plan personality description. When events didn't go to plan, were you acting against type?

ARE YOU EMPATHETIC?

Can you "get inside" someone's head, and imagine his or her thought processes, motivations, and feelings? Empathetic people can. They are good at thinking through how another person is feeling, and they do this by projecting their own thoughts and emotions into the situation, a similar process to acting. They use this special ability with everyone with whom they come into contact, friend or stranger, and use their insights to judge what to say to a person and how to say it. As a result, they often achieve a good outcome from social interactions, and are valued as friends. There is something inherently flattering and soothing about someone caring about how you feel and who understands your feelings.

For those of us who are less sympathetic, reading people's feelings can seem like a language we just don't speak. Why are they angry? Why don't they just get on with it? What did I do to upset them? Other people's behavior is a mystery. This is because unsympathetic people find it difficult to understand emotions unless they are actually experiencing them. Their reality is rooted in the here and now, and because they aren't upset or annoyed, they can't project how someone else feels. This makes them very straightforward and unmanipulative people, but they can cause aggravation and problems by not thinking before they speak or act.

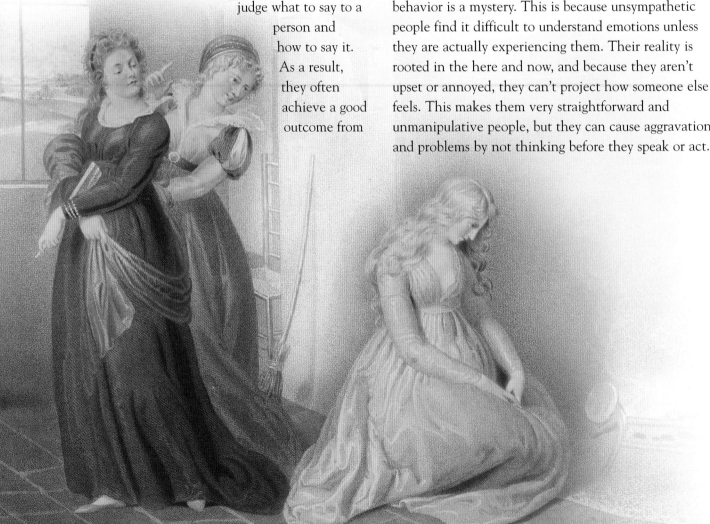

TEST YOUR INSIGHTS

Pick a fairy tale with several characters and a lively plot – something like Cinderella. Think through in your head who the main characters are in the story, and note them down, say the Ugly Sisters, the Stepmother, the Prince, the Fairy Godmother, and Cinderella. Using your knowledge of what they say and how they behave in the story, write about each character's feelings and motivations. Why do they behave the way they do? Why did they a take particular course of action? What could they be feeling?

When you have a complete character breakdown for each story member, consider whether you found the exercise easy or difficult.

SCORING/INTERPRETATION

If you found the exercise easy, you are empathetic because you were able to get in touch with the characters' feelings.
If you found it neither easy nor difficult, you are sympathetic.
If you found the exercise difficult, you are an unsympathetic type because you found it hard to get in touch with the characters' feelings.

If you are empathetic, you'll use your skills to your advantage. You will be good at negotiating, managing people or children, and dealing with the public, so jobs like teaching, team leader or tourist guide would be perfect for you. You are also likely to be in tune with your own emotions, because empathy with others involves putting yourself in their shoes. You should, however, guard against using this skill purely for your own ends – rather than making other people feel better – and becoming manipulative. Make sure you use your skills in situations where you have no particular interest in the outcome.

If you are sympathetic, you have a good combination of taking the direct approach and still being able to empathize. It's likely that some people are still unfathomable to you, but if you apply yourself you can deconstruct most situations. Try stretching your empathy skills – look for a supervisor's or management role at work, or do some voluntary work.

If you are an unsympathetic type, you'll fall into one of two groups. Either emotional insight passes you by and goes over your head, or you choose not to apply emotional insight because you don't see the point. In either case you'll probably feel that the straightforward approach to things is always the best, and your friends and colleagues will appreciate your directness. What's problematical is that you risk situations and events working against you, because you haven't got the full picture as to why someone is behaving the way he or she is. Try asking the person why he or she is upset or angry – you can feel sorry for him or her even if you don't fully understand it!

ARE YOU MODEST OR FORWARD?

The word "modest" is used in a number of different ways, but there is a common thread to the meanings: A modest portion, or a modest house, refers to something that isn't large or expensive; a woman may dress modestly to avoid unwanted attention, and a modest person does not boast about or make obvious his or her achievements – it is this meaning that applies to personality.

There is an irony surrounding modesty as a personality trait; we instinctively prefer modest people, yet the genuinely modest are often overlooked and forgotten in favor of those who shout louder.

Modest people believe that all people should be treated as equal and that too much emphasis is placed on status. They aren't in awe of anybody, and don't get a buzz from dealing with senior managers or meeting famous people. They accept people as they are, and are nonjudgmental. They are reserved about their achievements and avoid talking about themselves or their successes. They are willing to share credit for their success, and always publicly acknowledge help or support from others.

Forward people tend to talk about their achievements, and believe that keeping quiet about your ability or successes is like "hiding one's light under a bushel." They are less likely to share the credit for anything, and feel that the presentation of the facts is almost as important as the facts themselves. They believe that more senior people should be treated with respect, and they are concerned for their own status.

If you are a modest type, you'll be a quieter sort of person who is known for being self-effacing and egalitarian. You may be as ambitious as the next person, but you believe that actions speak louder than words, and you should be judged on your performance rather than the way you can talk it up. However, you may sell yourself short (or not sell yourself at all) and miss out on opportunities because less modest people edge in front of you and get themselves noticed. There is a fine but definite line between boasting and keeping quiet, and it's called the truth. If your achievements are true, speak up and enjoy the praise!

If you are an honest type, you sometimes put yourself forward, but the reasons for this vary. Some middle types are very insightful as to how and when they should speak out about their achievements; others are just not as outgoing as forward types, but have a slight tendency to praise themselves. Your aim is to develop the insight to know when to push yourself forward and when to be modest.

If you are a forward person, you are more likely to be outgoing and have a positive attitude to life. You believe that you need to promote yourself and present a positive image. But you are probably inclined to show off and pull rank over other people if you feel your status is higher than theirs. This will make you unpopular in the long run, so you need to curb this tendency. Try asking yourself how the other person would feel if you promoted yourself in this way: jealous, upset, belittled, proud, or impressed?

TEST YOUR MODESTY

Take a pen and paper, and a stopwatch or timer. Allow yourself 3 minutes to write about your successes, achievements, and special abilities or gifts, imagining you will be reading the list aloud to someone else. Start each sentence with "I can..." or "I have...", or "I am good at...".

Stop after 3 minutes.

SCORING/INTERPRETATION

If you found it challenging to express your good points and talents, and/or you came up with fewer than 10 sentences, you are a modest type.

If you struggled a little but started to get into the swing of things, and/or you came up with between 10 and 20 sentences, you are an honest type.

If you found it easy to express your good points and talents, and/or you came up with more than 20 sentences, you are a forward type.

DO YOU ENCOURAGE COOPERATION?

Imagine there is a proposition in your town for a new skateboard park for teenagers. Whose decision should it be whether the project goes ahead? Do you believe that all sections of society and interested parties should be consulted, so that as wide a range of views is obtained as possible? Or do you believe that some decisions are best made by a small number of well-informed, wise, and experienced local politicians, who best understand the consequences and costs of any decision?

These approaches to decision-making also scale down into everyday life. People with democratic personalities encourage other people to take part and participate; they consult with all those who may be affected, and listen to other people's views. This makes them considerate partners and family members, and popular team leaders at work. However, any popularity can

TEST YOUR IMPRESSIONS

The psychologist Hermann Rorschach developed "inkblot" tests in the 1920s. The test-taker looked at a series of symmetrical inkblot pictures, and was asked to say what they saw. The therapist used professional judgment to interpret these thoughts. This test uses an inkblot image, too. Look carefully at the image.

Now ask yourself:
Did you focus on the whole inkblot or specific parts of it? Do you think the individual splodges are facing inward or outward?

dissipate if a decision isn't made eventually – others will get fed up with what is perceived as dithering.

There are people who believe that the opposite style of operating bears the most fruitful results. Those with autocratic traits believe in taking control, and have faith in their ability to make decisions without long discussions with other people who may not be especially informed or interested in the topic. Have you ever had a debate with friends over which pizza to order, or restaurant to go to? In the end, one person decides and the party breathes a sigh of relief! The danger zone for this approach is that you may antagonize others, and resentment may build at their exclusion.

SCORING/INTERPRETATION

People who look at the whole inkblot pattern, and try to include every detail in their interpretation of the image, tend to look for similarities and ways to include others. People who focus on the individual details of the inkblot pattern, and perceive differences as separate features, tend to be self-sufficient and less group-orientated and inclusive.

If you focused on the whole inkblot, and thought the splodges were facing inward, you are a democratic type.
If you focused on specific parts of the inkblot, and thought the splodges were facing outward, you are an autocratic type.
If your responses were a mixture, you are a pragmatic type.

If you are a democratic type, your familial and social relationships are important to you, and you work hard to make sure everyone feels valued and is listened to. There's just one catch: you are unhappy making decisions unless you have the moral support of others. Start with something small (a surprise dinner party for a friend), and make a decision on your own; have the confidence to back it up and go with it.

If you are an autocratic type, you get frustrated by inaction and dithering, and are driven by a need to get things done. Your danger zone is that others you come into contact with feel unneeded, ignored, and demotivated. Practice asking the opinions of others. Write them down, and list one positive and one negative point for each. This will force you to pause and really consider other people's perspectives.

If you are a pragmatic type, you can be both a valuable group member and leader. You'll have learned that there are times when a consultative approach pays dividends, and times when taking the lead is critical to moving things forward.

WHAT'S YOUR RUNE?

Runes are a series of ancient symbols developed in Northern Europe that form an alphabet. The primary characteristic that distinguishes a runic alphabet from other alphabets is that each letter, or rune, has a meaning. For example, whereas "A" is just a sound denoting the first letter in our alphabet, the name of the first rune, "fehu," means "cattle" in the original Germanic language. Runes also have magical and religious significance as well, so the simple process of writing can be transformed into a magical spell. They are also used for divinatory readings, or for personal guidance. That guidance encompasses personality, character, and temperament, as well as past experience and behavior tendencies.

Runes fell into disuse as a language when the Roman alphabet became the preferred script throughout most of Europe, but their forms and meanings were preserved in inscriptions and manuscripts. Runes were commonly used for simple spells and consulting until the 17th century, when they were officially banned by the Catholic Church. The history and use of runes was revived by German academics in the 1920s and 1930s as part of the Nazis' interest in folklore, although much of the research was so influenced by Nazi ideology that it has been discarded. Runes became popular again in the 1980s as part of the resurgence of interest in "New Age" philosophies.

Today, runes have been rediscovered as a symbolic system and provide a key to understanding the lives and beliefs of the ancient people who created them. We can learn a great deal from runes about a way of life that was more closely connected to the natural world than our own. There are many ways of interpreting the runes, and ideally each rune should be carved on a small piece of wood so that the symbol can be held and a physical connection established.

The runic alphabet is traditionally divided into three families, or "aetts." The first aett contains the first seven letters of the alphabet, described in the chart, opposite.

SYMBOL	NAME
	Fehu
	Uruz
	Purisaz
	Ansuz
	Kenaz
	Gebo
	Wunjo

MEANING	INTERPRETATION
Cattle	Prosperity, money, wealth, physical and financial needs, goals, self-esteem, business success, promotion, finding a job, starting new enterprises
Aurochs (wild ox)	Energy, passion, vitality, instinct, wildness, sexuality, fertility, the unconscious mind, irrationality, rite of passage
Giant	Hardship, painful event, discipline, knowledge, introspection, focus, self-discipline, ending a bad situation, study and meditation
Odin (chieftain)	Authority figure, leadership, mind and body balance, justice, wise decisions, success, spiritual guidance, motivating, charisma
Torch	Wisdom, insight, solution to a problem, creativity, inspiration, enlightenment, studying and learning, dispelling anxiety and fear
Gift	Gift, offering, sharing, relationship, love, partnership, generosity, unexpected good fortune
Glory	Success, recognition of achievements, reward, joy, achievement of goals, contentment, motivation, completing or finishing

How can I use runes?

Sets of runes are widely available or you can make your own.

You may feel yourself drawn to a particular rune, and that may be because the symbol reflects your personality and best describes your beliefs, attitudes and intellectual make-up. That rune will help maintain your inner strengths and nourish you. Or it may be that the rune reflects an imbalance in your life – you are instinctively drawn to the rune which will give you strength to address your issues. Time and contemplation will reveal the reasoning behind your choice.

Keeping a favored rune in your pocket will give you strength during difficult meetings, encounters, or life events or you can use the name of your rune as a chant during meditation or for relaxation.

Similar to tarot cards, runes can be used for divination and personal guidance. You can scatter a selection of runes and interpret how they lie, or choose a few from a bag and reflect on their meanings.

ARE YOU CONSIDERATE TO OTHERS?

The ancient Chinese concept of Yin and Yang describes two complementary but opposing forces. Yin originally meant "the shaded side of the valley," and represents everything about the world that is subtle, passive, receptive, yielding, cool, soft, and feminine. Yang originally meant "the sunny side of the valley," and represents everything about the world that is evident, active, aggressive, controlling, hot, hard, and masculine.

Everything in the world can be identified with either Yin or Yang, although, in reality, both Yin and Yang are ever-present, one merely being dominant. The familiar diagram of Yin and Yang looks a little like two fish swimming around in a tight circle, and represents how Yin and Yang balance, oppose, yet can become each other. Each fish has an "eye" in the opposite color, showing that each contains a seed of the other. "Feminine" personalities can have an element of masculinity, and vice versa.

Consideration of others is a classic feminine, or Yin, personality trait, because traditionally it is the mother

TEST YOUR CARING QUOTIENT

Look at these pictures, and think about how they apply to your personality and the way you live your life.

Which of the two – the lion or the lioness – do you most identify with, and why?

who nurtures and cares for the family. While modern fathers may challenge this view, it still holds true for most of the animal kingdom. Caring people are good at looking after those in need, and are genuinely interested in the welfare of others. They help friends over difficulties, and show sympathy toward them. They are often asked for advice and are tolerant of different views and ways of life.

Indifferent people tend more toward Yang – they are not really interested in people's problems and feel uncomfortable talking about them. They feel that personal matters are best kept to oneself, and are less understanding when problems overspill into the work place or their social circle.

SCORING/INTERPRETATION

The lioness's role is to nurture and care for her cubs so that they grow into independent adult lions. If you feel you are more like the lioness, tending to look after people and things, then you are a caring type.

The lion's role is to be out there in the wide world defending his pride. If you see yourself as more of a lion, independent and disinterested in a caring role, you are an indifferent type.

If you saw elements of yourself in both the lioness and the lion, you're an interested type.

If you are a caring type, you'll take pleasure from helping and looking after other people. This might be your children, your family, your partner, friends, or colleagues. You would enjoy a job with a nurturing element to it: teaching, nursing, or therapy. You probably seek out needy causes as much as they seek your comfort and consideration. Your danger zone is that you live your life for others and through others, rather than for yourself. Try setting time aside for yourself and don't allow others to infringe it – take up a new pastime and make it "me" time.

If you are an indifferent type, you'll see other people's problems as their own to resolve and not really your business to become involved in. Neither do you share your problems with others, and would see that as a sign of weakness and a source of embarrassment. However, you're likely to live your life in your little cocoon, without reference to others less fortunate than yourself. Find a charity you believe in and support their work by getting involved.

If you are interested, you probably split your life, most likely caring at home and indifferent at work. Lots of people are loving and considerate partners and parents but see their professional lives as completely separate and do not like mixing the two. You might be missing out on valuable friendships at work by doing this. Try socializing with work colleagues occasionally to get to know them in a more relaxed atmosphere.

YOUR EXTERNAL TRAITS PROFILE

If you've completed all the external trait tests, you can profile your results to get an overall view of your "external" personality, how you relate to others, and your communication with colleagues, friends, family, peers, and partners. Circle the relevant boxes for each of your test scores, then add up the circled items you have in each column: A, B and C.

	A	B	C
Pages 68–69	Outspoken	Prudent	Quiet
Pages 70–71	Uninfluential	Plain-speaking	Persuasive
Pages 72–73	Compliant	Reasonable	Controlling
Pages 74–75	Reliant	Judicious	Independent
Pages 76–77	Gregarious	Amiable	Serious
Pages 78–79	Sociable	Agreeable	Aloof
Pages 80–81	Socially confident	Socially comfortable	Socially hesitant
Pages 84–85	Empathetic	Sympathetic	Unsympathetic
Pages 86–87	Forward	Honest	Modest
Pages 88–89	Democratic	Pragmatic	Autocratic
Pages 92–93	Caring	Interested	Indifferent
Total number	4	2	4

SCORING

If you have the most circled items in Column A, you are a typical extrovert.

If you have the most circled items in Column B or an equal number in any two columns, you are sociable.

If you have the most circled items in Column C you are an introvert.

INTERPRETATION

Extrovert

You love the company of other people, and get a real buzz from being with like-minded souls. You enjoy verbal banter, and see disagreements as a healthy and straightforward expression of views – nothing more. Team-work is a real skill at which you excel and, in fact, you feel uncomfortable working alone or without peer support. You can be a party animal when the mood takes you, and are good at raising morale. You have a talent for helping and nurturing.

Extrovert behavior has its downside, though. Others may find you too forthright, too verbal, too "in your face." You may misjudge situations because you get caught up in the excitement of the here and now, and assume that friends and colleagues are as open and easygoing as you are. You tend to put other people first, which means you miss out on potential opportunities.

Introvert

You are wary around strangers and people you don't know well. You need to feel relaxed in new social situations before you open up. You generally keep your opinions to yourself, and are careful about how you express them. You tend not to share your feelings readily or get involved in other people's problems. However, if others take the time to get to know you, you can be a discreet friend and partner, and can be trusted with sensitive information or gossip. You are able to distance yourelf from backstabbing or office politics, and this allows you to take a neutral stance on emotional issues. You are also a great organizer and manager, because you like being in control – of your emotions, other people, and any given situation.

You can, however, come across as unfriendly, aloof, and withdrawn, because you find it hard to make small talk at social events. This is often a misinterpretation, though, because you do enjoy social contact on your terms.

Sociable

You are able to adjust your style in your social interactions with others: You enjoy social events, but prefer smaller groups or more casual environments. You wouldn't really call yourself the life-and-soul of a party, but are good company when on form. You are assertive in your dealings with people, and encourage others to voice their views, too. You like to have a degree of control, but are willing to concede to someone more experienced or determined.

You are very likely to behave differently in your home than you do in your professional life – exrovert at home, introvert at work, or vice versa. This dichotomy can be hard to keep up, and you may find your double life difficult to maintain. You need to find the "real" person inside.

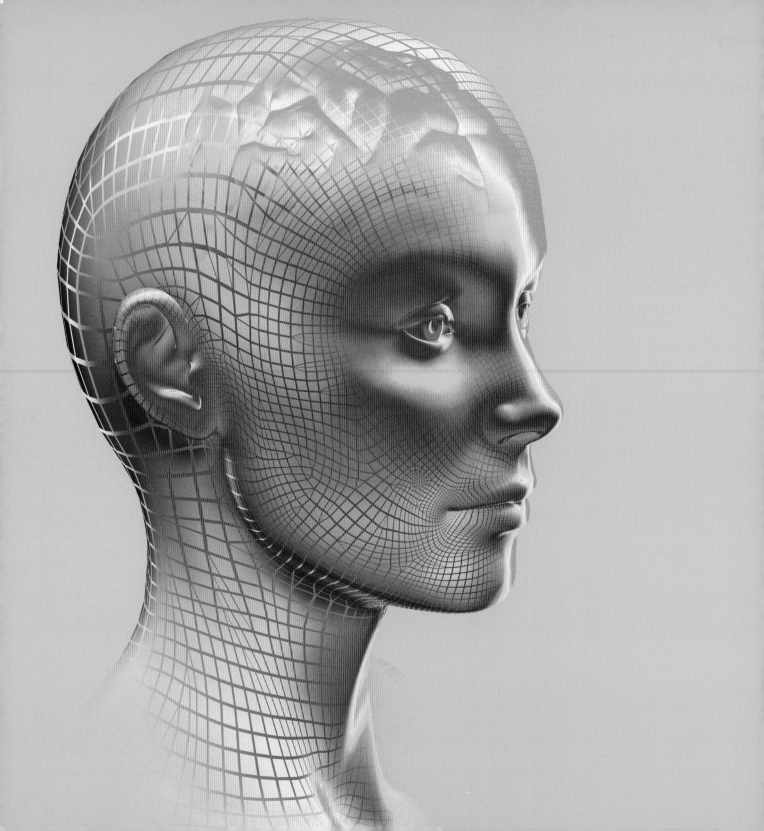

PART 3

INTERNAL TYPES

WHAT ARE INTERNAL TYPES?

The word "personality" comes from the word "persona," which originally were the masks used by Greek actors to portray different characters; eventually the word has come to mean "character" itself. Just as there are many different characters in Greek plays, personality can be seen as being made up of many different characters, or types. The theory is that these types are discrete and different from each other; you are mainly one or the other, not a little or a lot of all of them, as you are with traits. The Greeks themselves first sought to categorize personality by type. In 400 BC Hippocrates' theory of body humors was proposed, with just four types: melancholic, sanguine, choleric, and phlegmatic (see pages 40–41).

Type theories are popular across all the sciences; in biology, species and gender are type concepts, and in chemistry, the Periodic Table classifies elements by type. The debate within psychology has been whether human personality is really definable by type. Isn't such an approach just too simple? From a scientific point of view, it probably is simplistic, but from a popular perspective, the simplicity is part of the attraction. A single type is far easier to remember and understand than your profile in 16 or even 32 individual traits!

One popular self-development personality profiling system is based on internal type: the Enneagram (see page 9). The Enneagram is a both a visual symbol and a personality type theory. The symbol has nine points, corresponding to nine personality types, which also map onto each other to illustrate how the personality types interact. The Enneagram helps people to recognize and understand an overall pattern in human behavior through self-awareness and discovery, rather than a traditional psychometric technique. The nine personality types are particularly rich because they are described in terms of strengths and weaknesses, and "healthy" and "unhealthy" manifestations of each type. This broadens the opportunities for self-discovery and self-development.

This chapter contains tests that measure your internal types, those relevant to how you think and feel, what motivates and drives you. Make sure you read through the test instructions carefully, but don't spend too long thinking of an answer or the correct response – the first thing that comes into your mind is usually the most accurate reflection of how you are.

You may want to consider whether you are interested in discovering your type for self-knowledge or within a job context. Many people think and behave differently at home than they do at work: Generally the individual's "at home" persona is his or her true self, and the individual's "work" persona reflects how he or she would like others to see him or her. You might be an investigator at work, quietly capable and competent in your role, but an enthusiast in your private life, spontaneous and scatty. Or you might be an investigator at home and work, but find that the two different environments bring out "healthy" or "unhealthy" aspects of your particular personality type. Exploring your internal type will help you understand more about yourself, your motivations and talents. What type of person are you really?

Please note: This chapter contains simplified personality tests based on personality type theory. It is not a replacement for a professional Enneagram personality test or any other professional personality test, and the results are not intended to be the psychometric or practical equivalent to Enneagram assessment results.

ARE YOU A REFORMER?

No society stands still: times change, attitudes change, economics change. The outcome of change is eventually reform – the modification and restructuring of social institutions, with the aim of making them better. Prison reform, education reform, health reform, political reform … These topics are as current and popular today as they were 100 years ago.

So what sort of person initiates and drives reform? Well, someone with strong personal convictions, a sense of right and wrong, and personal and moral values. Reformers seek fairness, truth, and justice, and have the

TEST YOUR ZEAL FOR CHANGE

Read through these statements, and answer each with a "true" or "false" response:

1. There is always room for improvement. *TRUE*
2. I love getting involved in my community. *TRUE*
3. I find it hard to sit around and do nothing. *TRUE*
4. I am organized. *TRUE*
5. I believe in personal responsibility. *TRUE*
6. Change is important and usually makes things better. *TRUE*
7. I have strong morals and work ethics. *TRUE*
8. I often feel dissatisfied with something or other. *FALSE*
9. I will work long and hard to get the job done. *FALSE TRUE*
10. It's never OK to bend the rules. *FALSE TRUE*

ability to inspire others in their search for a better society. They have a very strong desire to "do good," and live their lives according to this mantra. Their Achilles' heel is that they can come across as self-righteous, inflexible, and critical, and feel dissatisfied and impatient with life and other people.

Reformers are drawn toward jobs that facilitate change for the better in society, often in the public sector, such as teaching, academic research, social work, and politics. In a business environment, they work hard, with a tendency to being "workaholics," and are self-controlled, organized, and principled. Once reformers are "off-duty" and in their home and community, they frequently get involved in local projects. They are hard-working committee members, and will seek to improve the life of everyone in the community.

SCORING/INTERPRETATION

If you answered "true" to 8 or more statements – you are a reformer.

If you answered "true" to between 4 and 7 statements – you are a secondary reformer.

If you answered "true" to 3 or less statements – you are probably the sort of person who is happy with the status quo.

If you are a reformer, you are conscientious and principled, and may be a religious person, or driven by a strong desire to make a difference and improve people's lives. Your danger zone is feeling that your way is the only right way, and you get frustrated by people who don't share your beliefs and values. Remember that reform is only possible through consensus, and that you need to get other people on board. Try taking a back seat and letting someone else lead on a project near to your heart.

If you are a secondary reformer, this means that you have a tendency toward reforming behaviors, but that it isn't your lead type. You don't quite have the drive, self-discipline, or perfectionist qualities of reformers, but you still enjoy changing your or other people's lives for the better. Perhaps you are happy in the tailcoats of a reformer; perhaps you have one key cause you feel strongly about for personal reasons.

If you are generally happy with the status quo, you tend not to initiate change so the reformers you know can appear humorless in their pursuit of their ideals, but now you'll understand this is a drive that is just part of their personalities. You can play this to your advantage, by getting a reformer to manage or take on a project they feel really strongly about, but make sure you agree on the desired outcome. This technique is good for channeling children's excess energies, if you can find a cause they can buy into.

DO YOU INFLUENCE PEOPLE?

Mentoring is increasingly used as a support and development process in businesses and organizations, as well as in educational contexts. Basically a mentor acts as a sort of trusted colleague and critical friend to someone new, less experienced, or needing to learn skills the mentor can impart. The role of the mentor is to support, guide, encourage, share knowledge, and help overcome obstacles and problems.

What sort of person makes a good mentor? Some people seem to have an innate talent for providing informal, yet insightful guidance. Mentors inspire trust and confidence, and are respected for their knowledge and ideas. They are thoughtful, encouraging, appreciative, generous, and compassionate. The same personality features apply to mentors in a general sense – they enjoy emotional closeness and like to please. They try to see the good in other people and like to get involved in their lives. The potential hazard for mentors is that they become meddling and interfering, and start to intrude.

Mentors are at their best when they have acquired valuable knowledge or expertise, and others seek to learn from them. They are patient parents, and enjoy helping their children gain new skills. Mentors make fabulous team leaders, and are natural coaches of new members of a club or society, ensuring everyone is included.

TEST YOUR MENTORING SKILLS

The story of the Mentor came from Homer's *Odyssey*. When Odysseus, King of Ithaca, went to fight in the Trojan War, he entrusted the care of his kingdom to Mentor who served as the teacher and overseer of Odysseus's son, Telemachus.

After the war and many years later, Telemachus, now a grown man, went in search of his father, accompanied by the goddess Athena who assumed the role of his mentor. Father and son were eventually reunited. Athena's role as mentor for Telemachus was not only to raise him, but also to prepare him for the responsibilities he was to assume in his lifetime. In time, the word mentor has become synonymous with a trusted friend, advisor, teacher, and wise person.

Set a timer for 10 minutes. Make sure you are familiar with the term "Mentor" and what it means. Write a list of the occasions when you have acted as a mentor to a child, friend, family member, or colleague. Stop when your time is up.

SCORING/INTERPRETATION

People who have the Mentor personality type find themselves naturally taking the role of Mentor in their relationships.

If you came up with 5 or more occasions when you acted as mentor, you are a primary mentor.

If you came up with between 2 and 4 occasions when you acted as mentor, you are a secondary mentor.

If you came up with only one or no occasions when you acted as mentor, you are a more *laissez-faire* personality type.

If you are a primary mentor, you need to feel loved and appreciated, and like to express your feelings for others. You have great interpersonal skills and are good at reading a situation and judging the best way to achieve the desired outcome. You appreciate the talents of others and often act as a confidante. You are good at networking.

If you are a secondary mentor, you may not be quite as skilled at bringing out the best in people, but you are naturally inclined to try. You are less likely to get bogged down in personal issues or manipulate people to achieve your end.

If you are more laissez-faire, you believe in leaving things alone and not getting involved. In your dealings with mentors – those who have trouble saying no to requests and tend to become stressed trying to help others too much – try not to overload them with tasks, even if they accept them willingly. They can also insist on exclusivity of friendship, which can be suffocating: if it bothers you, be sure to communicate your need for other friends.

Ayurvedic medicine has been practiced in India for over 5000 years: the ancient Sanskrit for "life" is "Ay" and "vedic" means "knowing." The basic philosophy is that our bodies are made up of the elements of water, fire, earth, space, and air. These five elements combine in pairs to form three dynamic interactions called doshas: space and air constitute the dosha Vata, fire and water combine to make up Pitta, and water and earth constitute Kapha. These doshas are constantly moving in dynamic balance with each other, influencing the physiology and psychology of our bodies and minds. We tend to have a dominant dosha, which reflects the characteristics, trait and tendencies we are born with.

DOSHA

Vata manifests itself as cold, light, rough, mobile, subtle, clear, dry, and astringent. The primary site of Vata is the colon. It also resides in the bladder, thighs, ears, bones and the sense of touch. The root "va" means "to spread" and it is responsible for all movement in the body, including the flow of breath and blood and the expression of speech.

Pitta is made up of fire and water. It is pungent, hot, penetrating, oily, sharp, liquid, spreading, and sour. Its primary function is transformation. It is the force of metabolic activity in the body associated with the endocrine function, hormone levels, digestion, body temperature, visual perception, hunger, thirst, and skin quality.

Kapha is a combination of the earth and water elements. It is slow, heavy, cool, dense, soft, oily, sticky, cloudy, liquid, and sweet. Kapha literally holds the body together. It is cohesive, gives shape and form, aids growth and development, lubricates and protects, helps smelling and tasting.

PERSONALITY

Vata personalities are enthusiastic, imaginative, talkative and energetic. They have difficulty making decisions because they have a tendency to worry and feel anxious about committing to the right way forward. Their danger zones are feeling afraid or insecure, and they are prone to mood swings.

Pitta personalities are efficient, perfectionist, persistent, and precise. They are full of opinions, and quite competitive. They are impatient and get irritated easily. Their downsides are feeling angry or irritated, or repressing their emotions.

The typical Kapha personality is relaxed, placid, methodical, and reliable. Kaphas are affectionate, forgiving, and enjoy their leisure time. Less favorable characteristics include being resistant to change and unconfident as well as greedy or possessive.

What can knowing my dosha do for me?

By identifying your primary dosha and understanding its characteristics, you can help your physical and emotional health by adjusting your diet.

Vatas thrive on sweet, sour, and salty foods eaten frequently in small amounts. Rich and warm foods and drinks also are tolerated. Vata should avoid astringent, bitter, and pungent flavors, because they all increase dryness. Heavy and infrequent meals are not recommended.

Pittas do best with cool foods and drinks. They can eat sweet, bitter, and astringent food such as salads. Pittas need to eat regular meals and can also tolerate rich foods. Their health is aggravated by pungent, salty, and sour flavors, because these increase heat. Hot and oily foods like garlic and fried foods also disturb Pitta. Infrequent and irregular meals and quick snacks should be off the menu, as should hot drinks.

Kapha is promoted by light, dry, hot food. Light meals including salads, soups and appetizer portions are beneficial. Pungent, bitter, and astringent flavors are well tolerated. Kaphas are aggravated by sweet, sour, and salty flavors, as they increase moisture. Kaphas should avoid cold foods and drinks, heavy meals, rich desserts, and between-meal snacks.

DO YOU PUSH YOURSELF AND OTHERS?

Motivation theory was the brainchild of Abraham Maslow, a sociologist. His "hierarchy of needs" claims all humans are motivated by needs, which start with the most basic – physiological needs (having food and water) and security needs (adequate housing and being safe) – and progress to more sophisticated ones – social needs (family and friends, being part of a community), esteem needs (recognition from peers, colleagues, or organizations), and the need for self-fulfilment (attempting or achieving personal goals).

Motivators as a personality type are operating at the esteem and self-fulfilment needs levels. They crave recognition for their achievements, and are careful about the image they portray. They have tremendous drive for self-fulfilment, and are constantly looking for ways to push themselves. They tend to set themselves personal goals, such as to climb a high mountain, or to win a prize, or to organize the most successful event.

Motivator types are also skilled at motivating others. They can be excellent role models, with the energy, drive, and ambition to bring others along with them. They lead by example, and seek out recognition for their team or organization as well as themselves. Motivators are born leaders.

TEST YOUR ENJOYMENT LEVEL

Consider each situation and decide if it would be pleasurable for you.

- Coaching a kids' sports team.
- Entering a painting in an exhibition.
- Being the lead presenter on a training course.
- Organizing a charity show in your community.
- Making and meeting New Years' resolutions.
- Coming up with ideas to improve morale in your team.
- Running a marathon.
- Encouraging colleagues to adopt a new procedure you've developed.
- Representing your organization at an exhibition.
- Starting a hobby club in your town.

If you are a motivator, you are competitive and love a challenge, especially if you can persuade others to take part. Social status and success are important to you because you like to be the best and to improve yourself. People are likely to have a high opinion of you.

If you are a secondary motivator, note whether the situations you identified as positive involve motivating yourself or other people – this will give you an indication of your strengths and natural tendencies. You are less likely to want to impress others or see your self-worth in terms of status.

If you are laid-back and relaxed, you are happy with how you are. You are unlike motivators, who may try to "package" themselves according to how they want to be perceived. With them, you have to dig a little deeper to find the real person. Their superficiality can cause motivators to lose touch with their true feelings, so encourage them to talk about their emotions.

IS YOUR HEART AN OPEN BOOK?

What does "romantic" mean to you? Many of us think of the special gifts or gestures that can demonstrate love for a partner. In 1969, Richard Burton bought the pear-shaped 69.42 carat Cartier diamond for Elizabeth Taylor, renaming it the Taylor-Burton. It became the ultimate and very public symbol of their love.

The Taj Mahal in India is traditionally associated with one of the most romantic (but tragic) love stores of all time. The Mughal emperor, Shah Jahan, and his favorite wife, Mumtaz Mahal, were devoted and inseparable, but she died soon after giving birth to their 14th child, and Jahan was so grief-stricken that he created the Taj Mahal as a mausoleum in her memory.

A romantic personality type goes beyond someone who just loves romance. As you might expect, romantic types are emotional people, who feel things deeply and sensitively. They often have jobs that exploit their creative, artistic, and dramatic abilities. Romantic people wear their hearts on their sleeves, and are good at communicating, listening, and being honest about their emotions and emotional needs. They can be temperamental and erratic, however, and expect others to accommodate their moods and habits. Romantics are good homemakers, with a flair for design and creating beautiful and aesthetic environments.

TEST YOUR WARM SIDE

Consider these childhood toys. Spend a few moments on each image, and let your mind wander. Which toy appeals to you most?

SCORING/INTERPRETATION

Which toy is your favorite?
Was it because:

It evoked powerful emotions in you? If you chose a toy because you liked the way it looked or the feelings it evoked, you are a romantic.

It is both attractive and functional? If you chose a toy because it was both attractive and functional, you are a secondary romantic.

It is functional, practical, and useful? If you chose a toy because of its function, you are an unsentimental type.

If you are a romantic, you are great with people because you are intuitive, emotionally literate, and communicative. You find criticism hard to take, although you can be self-critical and hard on yourself. You like to be surrounded by beautiful and stylish things, and love putting your personal "stamp" on your work, home, and life.

If you are a secondary romantic, this means that while you appreciate the aesthetic qualities of objects, their practicality also plays a role. You are less emotional and passionate than a primary romantic, and are more likely to disguise or deny your feelings. You are grounded and keep a hold on reality.

If you are unsentimental, you are a more down-to-earth person who does not get overly emotional. You find romantics emotional, tending to withdraw from people if they feel they are failing. Give romantics the space to pull themselves out of a mood, and let them know you are there for them when they want to talk. Don't get drawn into manipulative sulks or mind games.

DO YOU EXERCISE YOUR BRAIN CELLS?

Thinkers are tireless learners and experimenters, especially in specialized or technical matters. They like to understand in detail, spend time on research, and follow their curiosity wherever it leads. They are highly analytical and preoccupied with discovery, so time constraints and relationships can sometimes fall by the wayside. They also have a tendency to withdraw as they become absorbed in a task or project, and can appear secretive or as a loner. At their best, thinkers are visionary pioneers – perceptive, innovative and intellectually rigorous – bringing new ideas and profound depth to their work.

TEST YOUR ABILITY TO BUILD A BETTER MOUSETRAP

The archetypal profile of a thinker is that of an inventor, someone who can look at a problem differently, or can think of a new application or way of doing things. A notable example was Henry Ford (1863-1947). He started the Ford Motor Company in 1903 with the aim of building "a car for the great multitude" and produced the Model T. He achieved his aim by:

• Reducing the production time for a complete chassis from 728 minutes to

SCORING/INTERPRETATION

Did you find this activity easy? Did you enjoy the challenge of looking at a problem differently? If so, you are a primary thinker.

Did you begin the activity but got stuck in a thinking rut? If so, you are a secondary thinker.

Could you not even face starting the activity, and were tempted to turn the page? You are probably a down-to-earth individual.

93 minutes, by inventing a constantly moving assembly line, using subdivision of labor, and coordinating operations.

- Paying his employees $5 a day, double the wages offered by other manufacturers.
- Cutting the workday from 9 hours to 8 hours – so that he could convert the factory to a three-shift workday.

Think of a situation in your life or one you have come across that needs improving. It could be the organization of a neighborhood local festival, the time taken for your groceries to be scanned at the checkout, or the traffic jams on the freeway during rush hour. What would you do to change things for the better?

If you are a primary thinker, you observe everything with extraordinary perceptiveness and insight: nothing escapes your notice! You have good concentration, and love learning and gaining knowledge. Sometimes your innovation is a little too original for others, who may see you as whimsical and eccentric.

If you are a secondary thinker, you tried the activity but found it harder than you thought, you have the core features of a thinker personality, but enjoy the company of others too much to immerse yourself in anything too deeply. You may achieve innovation and invention through working as a team with friends or colleagues.

If you are a more down-to-earth individual, you are someone who is rooted in reality. You'll find that the thinkers you know tend to withdraw into themselves when they are absorbed in an activity or task, which has its downsides. At home, this can lead to emotional detachment and an increasingly complex inner world that isn't shared with you or the rest of the family. At work, the dangers are arrogance, poor communication with colleagues and intellectual bickering. If you are aware of these tendencies, you can help a thinker pull back from the brink of solitude.

CAN ONE COUNT ON YOU?

Loyalty is a much used word in business circles: every company wants loyal customers, those who return on a regular basis, trust the company to deliver on their promises, and spread positive messages about the company to their friends and neighbors. You may well be the holder of a "loyalty card" from a store, one that rewards you in some way for your continued custom.

Loyalty in personality terms is valued by us all as a character quality. Loyal friends and partners make us feel secure, special and supported. Loyalists are a personality type whose temperament is driven by loyalty: they are loyal to others and need to be shown loyalty in return. They need to trust people close to them, and feel secure and supported in their personal and professional lives. When this security is in place, they are lovable, appealing, and affectionate friends, companions, and colleagues. Loyalists form close bonds with others, and are dedicated to people and movements in which they believe deeply.

TEST YOUR COMMUNITY SPIRIT

There are many species, in addition to humans, which depend on and enjoy the support of others. Read through these descriptions of bees, and decide which category of bee you most resemble.

Category A bees live in large permanent families, or colonies, in which the queen and worker castes are markedly different in structure, each specialized for its own activities and unable to survive without the other. These bees build and maintain their hive, feed and nurture offspring, and store honey and pollen for food.

Category B bees may live in small colonies of two to seven bees of the same generation; one is the queen, or principal egg layer, and the others are workers. Such species form temporary colonies that normally break up in autumn, with only the fertilized queens surviving the winter. Bumblebees are a familiar example.

SCORING/INTERPRETATION

Bees are unusual in that some species are fully sociable, living in large colonies, while others are semi-social living in small colonies or in temporary colonies. The majority of bees, however, are actually solitary.

If you chose Category A, you are a social bee, and a primary loyalist, forming permanent, trusting, and mutually interdependent bonds with others.

If you chose Category B, you are a semi-social bee, and a secondary loyalist – cooperative and responsible, yet independent.

If you chose Category C, you are a solitary bee, and a changeable type, self-sufficient and autonomous.

Category C bees are mated females, each making her own nest in a burrow and storing provisions for her larvae. These bees tend to be specific to particular flowers, so, as soon as that flower's season ends, this bee dies as its food supply is cut off.

If you are a primary loyalist, you are a linchpin in your community: responsible and hardworking, encouraging a cooperative spirit. You need the security and support of friendships, and these enable you to bring out the best in others in return. Without this psychological buttress you feel insecure, anxious and volatile.

If you are a secondary loyalist, this means that the strengths and weaknesses of loyalists are less amplified in your personality. You are a little more self-supporting and have inner strength that doesn't rely on the input of others, but you are not as dedicated, selfless or positive as a loyalist on top form.

If you are an independent, you can appear fickle. Being part of a group is not that important to you, whereas the loyalists you know really rely on other people. Without this social support, they question their self-worth and may become self-destructive. You will get the best out of loyalists by encouraging and reassuring them.

DO YOU HAVE A RANGE OF INTERESTS?

Enthusiast is a term often applied to someone with a hobby he or she pursues with passion. Anyone who has a hobby knows what fun and pleasure this leisure-time activity adds to his or her life. Most hobbies provide opportunities to learn new skills that enhance our life experience, and add depth to our personalities, making us more interesting people to know. For some hobbyists, what they do is a vocation; for others, it is simply a source of considerable pleasure. They may use their leisure interests as means of winding down, or distancing themselves from their more mundane activities. The therapeutic value of hobbies is well recognized – people relax when they engage in leisure-time activities. The outcome isn't just the end result of the hobby – hobbyists also have enthusiasm, are creative problem solvers, have a zest for life, and a great sense of personal satisfaction.

TEST YOUR ANIMAL NATURE

Chinese horoscopes are based on twelve different animals which together reflect the whole spectrum of human behavior. Your animal influences your psyche, personality, and actions. Traditionally, your animal is assigned to the year of your birth, but an alternative and intuitive interpretation is to choose the animal with which you feel most aligned.

Three Chinese horoscope animals in particular reflect the spectrum of enthusiasm, in the personality sense of the word. Look at each image in turn, and then note to which animal you feel drawn. The feeling of identifying with a particular animal may happen immediately, or it may take several minutes. You may arrive at your decision by default, since not all of the 12 Chinese horoscopes animals are part of the test.

TIGER   RABBIT   OX

Enthusiast personality types share many of the personality features of hobbyists. They are busy, fun-loving people, enthusiastic about life and experiences. They are lively and vivacious, emotionally resilient, practical and productive. Enthusiasts find it easy to achieve accomplishment; they are multi-talented people who tend to do many different things well. They love the latest new gadget or trend, and can be impulsive shoppers. Their danger zone is the fear of being bored, so they can find it difficult to focus on mundane tasks, or to follow through an idea to its conclusion.

SCORING/INTERPRETATION

If you chose the Tiger, you are primarily an enthusiast. You are enthusiastic, powerful, affectionate, sincere, magnetic, optimistic, and lively. You can also be restless, quick-tempered, reckless, and demanding.

If you chose the Rabbit, you are a secondary enthusiast. You are diplomatic, happy, tolerant, honest, prudent, and attentive. You can also be superficial, pedantic, cunning, and sentimental.

If you chose the Ox, you are more stolid – responsible, loyal, methodical, trustworthy, self-reliant, and down-to-earth. You can also be slow, conventional, proud, and stubborn.

As an enthusiast, you are very likely to have at least one hobby, and have probably enjoyed a string of different interests in the past, moving from one new activity to the next. You may find this pattern repeated with job or careers; you need a challenge and thrive on developing new skills and gaining knowledge.

If you are a secondary enthusiast, you still enjoy new experiences, but appreciate what you have and tend to stick with what you know. You probably wouldn't call yourself an extrovert, although you do enjoy the company of lively and entertaining people.

If you are more stolid, you can seem indifferent, nonchalant, and apathetic. You can act in a way that makes enthusiasts feel trapped or cornered. They will have an infectious joie de vivre, which you may not appreciate and you may find them hyperactive and difficult to pin down.

DO OTHERS FOLLOW YOU?

We can all think of men and women who have been great leaders, although the names that first spring to mind tend to be political, religious, or business leaders on the world stage. These people have high profiles, and demonstrate clearly the core skills of good leadership: thriving under pressure, a clear vision for the organization, state, or country, and the ability to view a challenge positively. The role of emotional intelligence in leadership is crucial, too: Constructive criticism, feedback, and praise are all vital tools in motivating staff and improving their performance.

We've also all met great bosses – people who made us feel valued, understood, and promoted a culture of positive change – and lousy managers, people who were negatively critical, mean with praise, and disloyal.

Leaders as a personality type have a clear vision of what they want to accomplish and the willpower to make it happen. They make difficult decisions and see serious problems simply as challenges to be met and obstacles to be overcome. They love being in control and find it hard to delegate tasks or share leadership. They champion people, protecting and empowering them, but they can also be intimidating when they want their own way. At their best, leaders are magnanimous and generous, using their strength to improve others' lives.

Good leaders need to be tested, and thrive under pressure because it gives them an opportunity to really prove themselves. The pressure leaders come under has parallels in the natural world, in the formation of rocks. Just as with rocks, pressure causes us to react and shapes our characters.

TEST YOUR RESPONSIBILITY LEVEL

Chose the 5 statements which most apply to you:

1. I enjoy turning plans into reality.
2. People look up to me.
3. I like working in a team.
4. I get frustrated by people who cannot make decisions.
5. I like a relaxed and easygoing atmosphere.
6. I work well under pressure.
7. I find it difficult to criticize others.
8. I enjoy proving myself.
9. I tend to look for guidance when faced with difficulties.
10. I set myself targets.

SCORING/INTERPRETATION

If your top five statements were all the even-numbered items, you are a primary leader.

If your top five statements contained between 2 and 4 of the even-numbered statements, you are a secondary leader.

If your top five statements contained one or no even-numbered statements, you are probably a supporter.

If you are a leader, you are self-assertive, self-confident and strong, and can stand up for yourself and others. You like being the boss, and expect other people to support you and follow your lead. You can be intimidating and combative, and do not like backing down or having your authority questioned. You are courageous and resourceful, with a "can do" attitude.

If you are a secondary leader, you probably display the intrapersonal qualities of a leader – you are confident, decisive and have a passionate "inner drive" – but fewer of the interpersonal qualities of leadership, such as championing and commanding people, or trying to lay down the law. You are enterprising, individualistic, and determined.

If you are a supporter, you tend to seek guidance and direction from others and may feel let down if you are disappointed in their abilities. Leaders are at their most vulnerable when they feel they are being challenged or thwarted, so you can avoid petty point-scoring by being open and honest – but in private – if you have a disagreement. Bring out the magnanimous side of leaders by encouraging them to develop and nurture those who need help.

WHAT'S YOUR EGYPTIAN GODDESS?

The ancient Egyptians believed in many different goddesses (and gods) – over 2000 in all. Worshipping the deities was a large part of life in ancient Egypt, because the people believed that it was important to recognize, worship, and please these gods and goddesses so that life continued smoothly. "Official" goddesses of the state were worshipped by the pharaoh and priests in large temples; other goddesses were worshipped by ordinary people in their homes. Domestic goddesses were believed to protect people from the dangers of daily life, like scorpion bites, crocodile attacks, and the rigors of childbirth. Many of the goddesses had lots of duties and were combined with each other in a great number of ways. They could also appear in disparate forms; a goddess might have the head of a wasp and body of a hippopotamus. Goddesses are distinguished from gods by their legs: They are depicted with their legs together, whereas gods are shown striding with their legs apart.

Some goddesses took part in creation, some offered protection, and some took care of people after they died. Others were either local goddesses who represented towns, or minor goddesses who represented plants or animals. All aspects of daily life were covered by at least one of these deities, and like humans, they were members of families, who married and had children. Their personalities were made of both divine strength and human weakness, so ordinary people identified with them. Some were petty, or judgmental; others had terrible tempers and lost their tempers easily. They also did most of the things that ordinary people did, like harvesting, hunting, drinking, partying, and even dying.

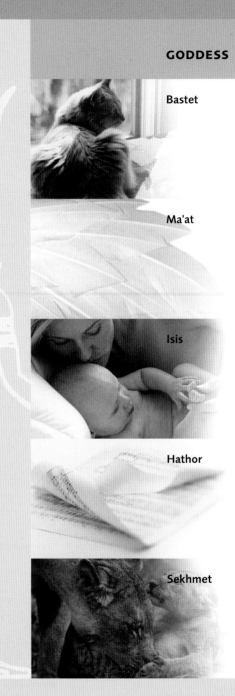

GODDESS

Bastet

Ma'at

Isis

Hathor

Sekhmet

DESCRIPTION	POSSIBLE MEANING
She protected pregnant women and was patroness for singing, music, and dancing. Protector of love, joy, and pleasure. Usually regarded as a gentle, protective goddess. Variety of depictions: head of a lioness, a woman with a cat's head, or as a sitting cat.	Nurturing, love, enjoyment, pleasure, leisure time, hobbies, relaxing.
Goddess of truth, justice, and harmony. Stood for good spiritual ideals and moral behavior. She was associated with the balance of things on earth. Depicted with feather of truth in her hair.	Inner strength, belief in ideals, truthfulness, judging other people, religious, spiritual.
A protective goddess who used powerful magic spells to help people in need. Stood for love, magic, motherhood, children, medicine, and peace. People asked her to make marriages happy. Depictions show associations with a throne.	Love, illness and wellness, motherhood, marriage, children, caring.
Patroness of music and dancing. Motherly figure. Protected the Pharaoh and helped him on his arrival at the afterlife. Connected with foreign places. Depicted with ears of a cow or headdress of horns and a sun disk.	Parenting, being a child, foreign travel, people from other countries, languages, music, and dancing.
The goddess of war, with the power to destroy Egypt's enemies, killing them with the rays of the sun. Sometimes connected with healing. She was shown as a woman with a head of a lioness to show her ability to be ferocious.	Arguments, speaking your mind, strength, cathartic honesty, pettiness.

What can a goddess do for me?

A goddess who reflects your personality will maintain your inner strengths and nourish you. She may indicate parts of your personality where you need a boost, and she will show you a path to self-development.

You can incorporate "your" goddess into your life in many ways. Here are some ideas:

• Each goddess is associated with an animal or object. Wear this as a charm on around your neck or wrist, or use it as a theme for a collection of objects in your home.

• Use the name of your goddess as a chant when meditating or feeling stressed.

• Find out more about your goddess. Try typing her name into an Internet search engine. Are there any temples to her still in existence? Was she the center of any cults? Which gods and goddesses was she related to?

• Find a picture or sculpture of your goddess and display her in your home.

PEACE OR WAR, WHAT'S YOUR CHOICE?

Peace generally has political connotations: while history is littered with seemingly irresolvable conflicts between peoples or nations, some of which have been going on for centuries, other conflicts, of both short or long duration, have been resolved against the odds, usually because a key figure acts as peacemaker.

Political peacemakers listen and try to understand a conflict from both perspectives. They are scrupulously fair, forgiving, just, and trustworthy. Peacemakers are patient, persevering, and open-minded, aware of the past but looking to the future with hope.

Personality peacemakers share many of these features. They have a harmonizing influence, and are good at bringing people together. They seem to have a healing or calming effect on warring parties, and are good mediators, communicators, and synthesizers of key issues.

Peacemakers aren't just concerned with harmony in their environments – they also seek inner "peace of mind." They tend to be unselfconscious, good-natured, and at ease with life and themselves. They try to avoid conflict and tension, to preserve things as they are, and to resist whatever would upset or disturb them. The downside of this behavior is that they are prone to wishful thinking, and hopelessly searching for magical solutions.

TEST YOUR RESPONSE TO INTERACTIONS

Look at these images of people interacting. Concentrate on each image for a few seconds, and make a note of the feelings it arouses in you, and the thoughts that are going through your mind.

If you are a peacemaker, you feel a connection to others, and a need to resolve any disagreements because you hate to see disharmony. Your strengths lie in negotiating peace between warring parties. However, be wary of trying to achieve personal peace at any cost – you have a tendency to avoid conflict in your relationships and not rock the boat for fear of a negative reaction.

If you are a secondary peacemaker, this may demonstrate itself through either your desire for inner peace, or your ability to help friends, family or colleagues sort out their differences. Because you aren't a primary peacemaker, there may be situations you just wouldn't want to get involved in.

If you are more confrontational, you probably feel comfortable with disagreement and debate. Peacemakers, on the other hand, try to protect others' feelings and may not always speak the truth. They are the ideal personality type to bring into a project where personalities have clashed, because they can smooth ruffled feathers with their healing and calming influence, but they need stability and do not react well to change, which makes them feel insecure.

SCORING/INTERPRETATION

Which standpoint is most similar to your thoughts and feelings?

(a) Did you feel upset by these depictions of discord – were you curious why the people were arguing? Did you want to wade in and try to resolve their differences? If so, you are primarily a peacemaker.

(b) Did you feel neutral about the scenes – whatever they are arguing about is nothing to do with you? If so, you may be more confrontational.

(c) Neither (a) nor (b) – sort of in between. If so, you are a secondary peacemaker.

YOUR INTERNAL TYPE PROFILE

If you've completed all the internal type tests, you can profile your results to get an overall view of your "internal" personality; how you think, feel, learn, and love. Circle the relevant boxes for each of your test scores, then add up the circled items you have in each column: A, B and C.

	A	B	C
Pages 100–101	Happy with Status Quo	Secondary Reformer	Reformer
Pages 102–103	Primary Mentor	Secondary Mentor	Laissez Faire
Pages 106–107	Laid-back	Secondary Motivator	Motivator
Pages 108–109	Romantic	Secondary Romantic	Unsentimental
Pages 110–111	Down to Earth	Secondary Thinker	Primary Thinker
Pages 112–113	Primary Loyalist	Secondary Loyalist	Independent
Pages 114–115	Enthusiast	Secondary Enthusiast	Stolid
Pages 116–117	Supporter	Secondary Leader	Leader
Pages 120–121	Peacemaker	Secondary Peacemaker	Confrontational
Total number			

SCORING

If you have the most circled items in Column A, you are a networker.

If you have the most circled items in Column B or an equal number in any two columns, you are independent.

If you have the most circled items in Column C, you are a leader.

INTERPRETATION

Networker

You have tremendous interpersonal skills but you need to feel loved, to express your feelings for others, and like to be appreciated. You are intuitive, good at reading a situation, and reacting or speaking accordingly to get the best outcome for all concerned. You love working with others, finding new friendships, and being a part of your community.

Your weakness lies, too, in your relationships with others. You really need the security and support of friendships, and without them feel insecure, anxious, and volatile. You find criticism hard to take, and have a tendency to avoid conflict and "rocking the boat" at any cost, because you don't want to lose a friend or valued colleague.

Leader

Conscientious and principled, people generally have a high opinion of you. You are introverted, and your personality is driven by an inward-looking and somewhat egocentric approach to life. You are competitive, self-confident, and love a challenge. Because you don't feel the need to be friends with everyone you work with, people consider you a natural leader. You are courageous and resourceful, with a "can do" attitude.

What is your downside? You feel that your way is the best way, and you can be intimidating and combative. You don't like backing down or having your authority questioned, and get frustrated when people don't share your beliefs and values. You may resort to forcing through change or decisions, and have to work hard at your "people skills."

Independent

You will enjoy the company of other people, but need time alone to recharge your batteries. You probably wouldn't call yourself an extrovert, although you do enjoy the company of lively and entertaining people. You are confident and determined, and don't feel the need to impress others, nor do you see your self-worth in terms of status. You aren't especially emotional, and are able to disguise or deny your feelings to suit the situation.

What are your weaknesses? Well, while you like being part of a team you aren't really skilled at bringing out the best in people. You have a tendency towards superficiality, flitting from one idea or person to the next without thinking about anything too deeply, not feeling anything too strongly, and getting bogged down in detail. You may hang onto someone else's tailcoats as a quick-fix way of achieving something or getting noticed.

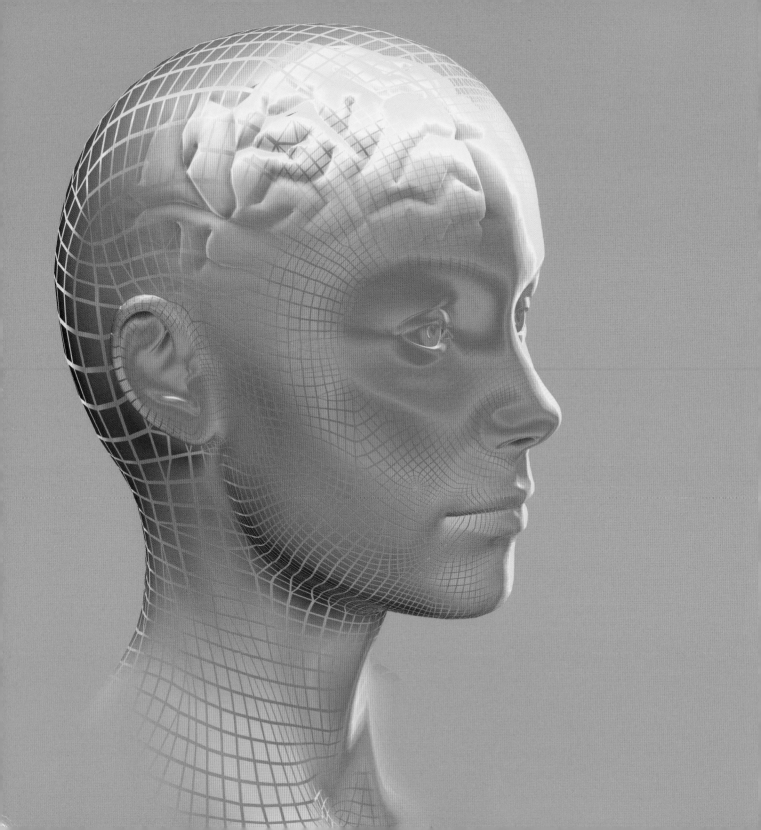

PART 4

EXTERNAL TYPES

WHAT ARE EXTERNAL TYPES?

Personality is such a broad description of our persona, or psyche, that psychologists have sought for centuries to find ways of categorizing and defining it. The two main methods are by trait and by type. Type theories are based on the premise that personality can be seen as being made up of many different characters, or types. The theory is that these types are discrete and different from each other: You are mainly one or the other, not a little or a lot of all of them, as you are with traits.

Some of the world's best-known personality team-building tests are based on external types, or include measurement of them in the questionnaire. One of these is the Belbin Team Roles, developed by Meredith Belbin to define and predict potential success of management teams. Belbin recognized that the strongest teams have a diversity of characters and personality types. He defined a team role, or type, as "a tendency to behave, contribute, and interrelate with others in a particular way" and identified nine separate roles.

Elements of external type theory also form part of the Myers-Briggs Type Indicator (MBTI), another famous and popular personality test. Reported to be used by 89 of the Fortune 100 companies in the US for hiring, training, or team-building purposes, it is based on Carl Jung's notion that people function in the world in four main ways, and the questionnaire forces you to choose from two opposing options to arrive at your profile (Introversion/Extroversion, Intuition/Sensing, Thinking/Feeling, Judging/Perceiving), so you might be "INTJ" or "ESFP," for example.

One of the criticisms of type theories is that they put people into boxes or pigeonhole them and thus over-simplify personality. Psychologists would probably agree, but the usefulness of knowing your type as opposed to those of people around you has ensured their growing popularity. A single type is far easier to remember and understand than your profile in 16 or even 32 individual traits! It's common for people who know their Myers-

Briggs profile to cite it to colleagues or even friends and family, and a lively debate often ensues.

This chapter contains tests that measure your external type, those relevant to how you think and feel, what motivates and drives you. Make sure you read through the test instructions carefully, but don't spend too long thinking of an answer or the correct response – the first thing that comes into your mind is usually the most accurate reflection of how you are.

You may want to consider whether you are interested in discovering your type for self-knowledge or within a job context. Many people think and behave differently at home than they do at work: Generally a person's "at home" persona is his or her true self, and the individual's "work" persona reflects how he or she would like others to see him or her. You might be a Performer at work, known for your love of fun and upbeat sense of humor, but a Resource Investigator in your private life, helping your local school find funds for new equipment.

Exploring your external type will help you understand more about yourself, your motivations and talents. What roles do you play?

Please note: This chapter contains simplified personality tests based on personality type theory. It is not a replacement for the full Belbin® or Myers-Briggs® questionnaire or any other professional personality test, and the results are not intended to be the psychometric or practical equivalent to Belbin® or Myers-Briggs® questionnaire results.

ARE YOU A RESOURCEFUL PLANT?

Think of a weed growing in your backyard or the park, sprouting from a wall or sidewalk. What sort of positive personality features would you ascribe to it? How about self-sufficient, opportunist, determined, a survivor? Weeds manage to take root in meager surroundings, looking after themselves (they never need watering, do they?), and may surprise you with their tenacity and drive to thrive, using whatever means they can.

Now imagine a plant as a team member. A plant is essentially someone who is good at taking action, and enjoys solving problems creatively. Plants will take risks, and often approach tasks in an unusual or unconventional way. They help smooth over stumbling blocks but their danger zone is that they can be too preoccupied with their own work to communicate

TEST YOUR REACTIONS TO MANTIS

African Bushmen tell stories of Mantis, a sort of "super-being" with the personal qualities of Bushmen themselves. In many ways he also personifies Plants: imaginative, courageous, unorthodox, and good at solving difficult problems.

Before people had fire, they ate their food raw like the leopard or lion, and they spent their evenings in cold darkness, with no warming light to brighten the long dark hours. Mantis noticed that Ostrich's food smelled different and delicious, so one day he crept close to Ostrich to watch him eat.

He saw Ostrich furtively take some fire from underneath his wing, and dip his food in it. When he had finished eating, he carefully tucked the fire back under his wing and walked away.

Mantis knew that Ostrich wouldn't share his fire, so he made a plan. He went to visit Ostrich and called to him. "Come," he said, "I have found a tree with delicious plums on it." Ostrich was delighted and followed Mantis, eating the plums that were easiest to reach. "The best plums are right at the top!" encouraged Mantis, and as Ostrich stood on tiptoe he lost his balance and used his wings to steady himself. Mantis snatched some of

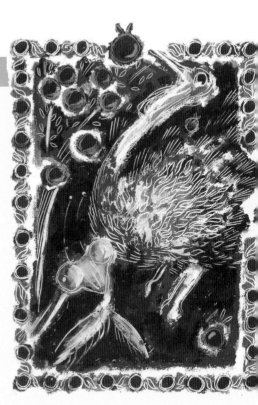

effectively. They have a tendency to ignore incidentals and don't worry about breaking rules in order to get things done.

Plants are valuable team members if the project or task is difficult, or getting held up by annoying glitches. As an individual, a plant is best personified by his or her problem-solving skills. Imagine hosting a dinner party when an extra guest arrives ... Setting out on a car journey and getting stuck in a traffic jam ... Working out why the vacuum cleaner keeps getting blocked ... Getting the kids to stop fighting and start playing ... A plant would probably come up with original and working solutions to these issues.

the fire from beneath his wing and ran off.

This is how Mantis brought fire to the people. And since then Ostrich is so ashamed at being tricked that he has never flown, and keeps his wings pressed close to his sides to preserve the little fire he has left.

Do you believe that Mantis
(a) Did a great job in outwitting Ostrich to achieve his aim?
(b) Achieved his end results successfully, but through rather questionable means?
(c) Is a trickster, without morals or scruples?

SCORING/INTERPRETATION

If you answered (a), you are primarily a plant.

If you answered (b), you are a secondary plant.

If you answered (c), you are more likely to be an implementor or specialist.

If you are primarily a plant, you'll enjoy doing things spontaneously, and have hobbies and interests that reflect your creativity and imagination. You are the sort of person who has loads of ideas. You dislike constraints, excuses for inactivity or results, and too much talk. You believe that if you don't like something, or it doesn't work, you should do something about it, whatever the consequences.

If you're a secondary plant, you could assume the role of plant, or adopt these sorts of tactics if required, although it doesn't come completely naturally. You are least comfortable with breaking rules for the sake of expediency or the greater good, and are more conventional than true plants.

If you are an implementer or specialist, your gifts lie in other areas, see pages 136–137. Give plants something creative to do, and make sure you keep open the lines of communication as they may forget to keep in touch once absorbed by something.

ARE YOU A COORDINATOR?

Are you one of those people who like your clothes or home furnishings to coordinate? Do you have matching accessories, or enjoy creating a decorating style where each element complements the others? If so, the chances are that you have an innate desire and ability to bring objects together, the vision to see what they have in common, and to get them to work together in harmony.

Coordination also applies to people. Coordinator types excel in finding the common factor in people, and are good at getting them to gel together. They are particularly skilled at getting people to work together for common goals, and are good at spotting and developing individual talents. People tend to think of coordinators in a corporate setting, but they use their skills in all sorts of other environments. This can take the form of supporting a partner, nurturing children, encouraging community spirit, managing a sports team, or leading an organization.

TEST YOUR RECEPTIVITY

Consider these objects. Spend a few moments on each image, and let your mind wander. What do you find yourself thinking or doing?

If you are primarily a coordinator, your talent is in being able to get other people to work towards shared goals. You'll enjoy getting the best out of people, and feel a real sense of achievement in effective team-working. You tackle problems calmly and effectively, but there is a lazy side to you that feels that if you can get someone else to do something you will.

If you are a secondary coordinator, you may well have taken on the role of coordinator in a team, although it doesn't come completely naturally. You enjoy being part of a team, and getting it working well, but you probably feel less comfortable leading it.

If you are an implementer or a specialist, your talents lie in other areas (see pages 136–137). But if you are managing a coordinator, ensure he or she is pulling his or her weight; if you have one in the family, give him or her an organizing task, which will play to his or her skills.

Coordinators are people-orientated, mature, and confident. They are good at clarifying goals, promoting decision-making, delegating, and empowering others. They tend to be respected by others for their experience and broad outlook on life. They are excellent homemakers, team leaders, and committee heads. But you'd be surprised if they didn't have a weakness, wouldn't you! Coordinators can sometimes be seen as manipulative because they are so good at getting others to do what they want, and have a tendency to delegate their own work or tasks to others rather than buckle down themselves.

SCORING/INTERPRETATION

Did you try to form associations between the items, such as noting that the pen and feather can both be used to write on the notepad, or that the cup and the car both start with the same letter? If so, you are a primary coordinator.

Did you find that some associations popped into your mind, but you didn't seek to link every item in some way? If so, you are a secondary coordinator.

Did you focus on the objects as individual items, perhaps noticing their colors, features, or remembering a toy you loved as a child? If so, you are more likely to be an implementer or a specialist.

CAN YOU WEIGH UP THE OPTIONS?

Question: what have these people got in common? A judge presiding over his court, ensuring fairness in a libel trial. A mother whose kids all want something different to eat, but she manages to get them to agree to her cooking only one thing. A colleague who steps in and convinces two project managers who don't see eye-to-eye on the best way forward for a project. A man buying a new bed in a department store, carefully checking the size, firmness, price, and specification so he can make an informed choice. Answer: They are all displaying the qualities of monitor-evaluators.

Monitor-evaluators are very good at weighing up the facts, carefully considering the pros and cons of each

TEST YOUR DREAM INTERPRETATION

Here are some common dreams. Consider each scenario, and answer each question.
Make a note of your responses.

Dream 1 You are flying through the air like a bird, looking down on your life below.
Question A: How do you feel?
(a) Out of control.
(b) Free.
Question B: What do you think it means?
(a) Something to do with being changed or not being myself.
(b) Something to do with escaping reality.

Dream 2 You are talking to your partner and your teeth start to feel loose in your mouth. They then fall out.
Question A: How do you feel?
(a) Terrified.
(b) Frustrated.
Question B: What do you think it means?
(a) Not being able to say what you mean.
(b) Fear of being humiliated.

Dream 3 You are driving through the night and realize you have arrived again at your childhood home.
Question A: How do you feel?
(a) Intrigued.
(b) Swamped by memories.
Question B: What do you think it means?
(a) Something bad to do with my parents.
(b) Not being able to move on with my life.

option, and finally coming to a well-considered decision. This is commonly a very objective process, free from influence of emotional factors. They have a certain detachment that can be critical in emotive situations, but exasperating to those involved who may view this detachment as indifference. The key to successful monitor-evaluators is that they maintain a backseat role, and then step into the limelight when a crucial decision needs to be made. In many ways, the lack of commitment to team goals facilitates the task of the monitor-evaluator because this enables him or her to be impartial in decision-making.

SCORING/INTERPRETATION

Monitor-evaluators are good at sitting back and concentrating on the facts, rather than letting emotional factors influence their judgment or thinking. Our dreams are often bizarre, frightening or make us anxious if taken at face value, but with a little detachment and analysis, an alternative and non-literal interpretation may prove enlightening. Flying is often interpreted as a need to get away from everyday life and be yourself, shedding teeth as problems with having one's voice heard or being understood, and revisiting the past indicates you are in a rut and repeating mistakes or patterns of behavior. Monitor-evaluators are more likely to see beyond the literal; other types find this harder.

If your answers contained 5 or 6 (b)s, you are primarily a monitor-evaluator.

If your answers contained 3 or 4 (b)s, you are a little analytical with a tendency for emotive interpretations, and are a secondary monitor-evaluator.

If your answers were mostly (a)s, you look at dreams emotionally, and are more likely to be a coordinator or performer.

If you are a monitor-evaluator, you are intelligent, discerning, and objective, and are respected for your sound judgment. You aren't particularly creative, enthusiastic, or personally committed, but this actually enhances your status as an impartial decision maker. You'll enjoy a hobby or work situation which plays to your intellectual and analytical strengths.

If you are a secondary monitor-evaluator, you may step into the role of monitor-evaluator, but it would take a conscious decision rather than a natural tendency. It probably won't feel totally natural or comfortable, either, because you are more likely to be emotionally involved in the thick of things.

If you are a coordinator or performer, your personality shows other tendencies (see pages 130 and 140). The main thing to remember about monitor-evaluators, if you work or live with them, is that they are observers rather than partakers – but at the first sign of difficulty, they can help show the way forward.

WHAT DOES YOUR HANDWRITING REVEAL?

In 1875, the French Abbot, Jean Hyppolyte Michon, coined the phrase "graphology," from the Greek: "graph" meaning, "to write" and "logos" meaning "theory." Although the term graphology is relatively recent, the subject itself dates back many centuries, having originally been taken from Southern India to China and from there to Greece, circa 2000 BC.

Graphology is essentially the study of personality through the analysis of handwriting. It is based on the premise that as soon as someone has learned to write, following the ability successfully to copy and reproduce prescribed letter forms from memory, he or she gradually alters the shapes and sizes of the letters (without necessarily reducing the legibility of the script). This is not done in a haphazard manner as one might at first imagine, but strictly in accordance with individual likes and dislikes. It has even been shown that if a person loses the use of his or her writing hand and is forced to use the opposite hand, the same basic tendencies will appear in his or her writing – so if you loop your letter "y," this tendency will manifest itself eventually whichever hand you write with.

Handwriting can vary from day to day and, to a certain extent, reflects the mood of the moment. However, many elements remain constant and these give an accurate reflection of underlying personality. Graphology can also reveal unconscious anxieties, which are an important factor and may be holding the individual back from achieving.

"It has long been accepted by all societies that the signature of a man can be used to identify his transactions: this signature is now accepted by law, on bonds, deeds, and other official documents. If you make an affidavit for a Court of Law, you confirm it with your signature. By writing your signature on a check you dispose of your own money. To forge another person's signature is a crime heavily punished by the criminal law of every country."

DR ERIC SINGER

THE ANALYTICAL ELEMENTS

In looking at a piece of writing, first of all, the overall style is examined:

Little space between words	Loves company and having lots of people around
Wide spaces between words	Happy being alone
Irregular and illegible	Colorful but unpredictable
Write with heavy pressure	Great energy, but can get stressed
Large writing	Sociable
Uneven baseline	Open to suggestion, good listener
Mixed slant	Tendency to be moody
Vertical slant	Straight-talking, honest, not overly-emotional
Left slant	Needs security

This is followed by an analysis of how individual letters are constructed and words formed:

Loops on letters g and y	Caring and loving
Long "t" bars	Hardworking, determined to succeed
Connected letters	Well-organized, doesn't like surprises
Disconnected letters	Intuitive, knows what others are thinking or feeling
Letters squashed together	Shy, worried about making a good impression
Printed letters	Attention-seeking
Long stick-like strokes	Stubborn, argumentative

An overall picture of personality is then built up.

What can graphology "tell" me?
Graphology has traditionally been used as a personality assessment in recruitment and job selection. Some people find it valuable in personal therapy and vocational guidance. Here are some ways in which it can provide useful information.

• Make regular samples of your handwriting – perhaps diary entries. At times of stress, re-analyze your writing for signs of change. Your writing may alert you to issues of which you haven't become consciously aware.

• Get together with friends and compare your handwriting samples. Interpret each other's writing style and letter formation, and take a vote on the accuracy of the readings.

• You will find samples of celebrities' handwriting on the Internet, often accompanied by interpretations from expert graphologists. Compare your analyses with theirs.

• Try writing with your non-preferred hand. Practice regularly and compare your left and right handwriting samples. Note any similarities or differences.

DO YOU MAKE THINGS HAPPEN?

How would you feel if you were asked to follow through someone else's plans? If you were given a concept or idea and asked to turn it into practical actions? If you are an Implementer, you'd love it! Implementers would be great assets in situations such as assembling a new flat-pack wardrobe from the instructions, coordinating an annual school fund-raiser, following company guidelines on procedures, directing a team of volunteers at a homeless shelter – all situations where you need to be organized, prepared to work hard, and interested in the details of the task.

Implementers are disciplined, reliable, efficient, and in control of their emotions. They stick to plans and agreed or standard processes, and work through their tasks systematically and conscientiously. They prefer order and routine, which may result in a slightly inflexible or plodding approach. The other downside of implementers is that they aren't original thinkers or spotters of new opportunities; rather, they are excellent at implementing schemes other people have devised.

TEST YOUR PART IN THE PROCESS

Take a few minutes to look at this building and the architect's plans that accompany it. The process starts with the client, the person for whom the building is being created. His or her wishes, lifestyle, and fantasies are turned into detailed plans by the architect, the person who interprets the client's brief into practical plans. Finally, the site manager directs the building site and turns the plans into reality. Think about the process and where you would see yourself fitting most naturally. Which role – the client, the architect, or the builder – suits your personality best?

If you are a primary implementer, you get a thrill from working through tasks methodically and being the last port of call in making a dream happen. You'll enjoy a job where a formula, guidelines, or plan already exists and where you can direct and encourage others to achieve a successful outcome. You have a strong work ethic.

If you are a secondary implementer, chances are you enjoy being part of the planning process, and are able to work in a more chaotic environment than a primary implementer. You still can work systematically and steadily, but also have a creative streak. Play up this side of yourself when job seeking; people who get the job done are popular employees.

If you are a plant or a resource investigator (see pages 142–143), you will have a different take on making things happen. When you meet someone who follows rules, applies himself to any task, and works hard, you know you've met an implementer. He doesn't like generating new ideas and would rather have strict parameters about what is expected of him.

Implementers are driven by a strong work ethic, and are often left to cope with aspects of work that other people find difficult or undesirable. They are therefore extremely valuable team members, particularly when complemented by more creative, free-thinking types.

SCORING/INTERPRETATION

Are you like the client – enthusiastic, inspired with new ideas, a creative thinker unconstrained by what is realistic or practical? If so, you do not have Implementer tendencies and are more likely to be a plant or resource investigator.

Are you like the architect – able to crystalize ideas into actual plans, injecting some practicality, but leaving others to actually carry things out? If so, you are a secondary implementer.

Are you like the site manager – capable of great organization, directing subordinates, problem solving and gaining satisfaction from working through plans to achieve a successful outcome? If so, you are a primary implementer.

CAN YOU WRAP UP THINGS?

How would you feel if a protracted, difficult, and time-consuming project you were involved in collapsed? You might feel relief that you no longer had to struggle with clashing personalities and deadlines or, might you feel intensely frustrated that your time and efforts amounted to nothing? What would you do if you were following a recipe and discovered halfway through that you lacked a vital ingredient? Would you forget the whole thing, or change tack and use a different recipe? Or, might you rush out to buy what you need to complete the recipe?

Completer-finishers are the sort of people who feel cheated at not achieving the successful and final outcome they had envisaged. They are hardworking and conscientious, and are good at planning and paying attention to detail. They tend to work through issues logically and methodically, and are suited to searching out errors and omissions. They deliver on time, and are organized and self-disciplined.

Are there any negative sides to completer-finishers? You bet! We know that they are tenacious, but there are occasions when they refuse to accept defeat or a shift in direction because they view this as failure. They are very reluctant to let a matter drop unresolved if it is important to them. They can be a little anxious, too, almost as if they can't relax until a project or task has been completed to their satisfaction. But on the whole, a completer-finisher is a great person to have around.

TEST YOUR IDEAL STYLE

Spend a few moments looking at these drawings, thinking about the illustration style and which you feel best reflects your personality.

SCORING/INTERPRETATION

Do you prefer the detailed illustration, because it is a complete representation of the subject? If so, you are a primary completer-finisher.

Do you like the sketchy illustration, where much of the image is left unfinished, and the bird's outline is only "suggested"? If so, you are more likely to be a coordinator or implementer.

Do you find yourself drawn to the more impressionistic style, where a little is left to the imagination but the image is still quite clear? If so, you are a secondary completer- finisher.

If you are a completer-finisher, you are good at tying up loose ends because you are organized, have an eye for detail, and stick to plans and schedules. You'll enjoy tasks that you can see through to the finish, and hobbies that involve art and crafts, where a final outcome is achieved – a beautiful object created. You tend to keep your emotions in check, and aren't particularly extravert.

If you are a secondary completer-finisher, you can take on the role of a completer-finisher within a group or team, but it isn't what drives you. You might work consistently and methodically to aim for solid success, or try an opportunistic approach with spectacular but riskier success in mind.

If you are a coordinator or implementer (see pages 130–131 or 136–137), you will approach things very differently. If you have a team or group that is heavy on enthusiasm and somewhat light on experience or steadiness, choose a completer-finisher to create balance.

ARE YOU A PERFORMER?

Sportspeople, musicians and artists are all judged on their performance – the way they conduct themselves in a particular day in front of an audience. Concert musicians, for example, use both physical and mental techniques for ensuring their performances reflect the best of their abilities. They often try to calm their breathing and relax to ensure their bodies aren't over-hyped, which can affect memory and fine motor skills. They mentally prepare by visualizing a fantastic performance where every note went to plan, and use positive self-talk to buoy themselves up and put themselves in a good frame of mind.

"Performing" is also a personality type. These people enjoy performing and demonstrating their abilities, and they strive to achieve the best they can. They have strong internal drive, and come into their own when an element of performance is required, such as making a key presentation or staging an event. They are exceptionally in tune with their senses, and use sound, visual elements or physicality to reach their goals. There is a flip side to performance: The need to be admired and liked. Performers love entertaining team members, and keep morale up by telling jokes, singing, or acting the fool. This can make them appear flippant, and can be a source of irritation to others.

TEST YOUR DRIVE TO PERFORM

Read through these statements, and answer each with a "true" or "false" response:

1. Sometimes I behave, dress or speak a particular way just to be noticed.
2. I love being the center of attention.
3. I am a pretty confident person.
4. I feel in control of my body.
5. I set myself targets and goals.
6. Life is enriched by the arts.
7. I believe you have to work hard and long to achieve results.
8. I think about my image and how I present myself to other people.
9. I enjoy participating in the theater, dance shows, or sporting events.
10. I find it very upsetting if someone doesn't like me.

SCORING/INTERPRETATION

If you answered "true" to 8 or more statements – you are a primary performer.
If you answered "true" to between 4 and 7 statements – you are a secondary performer.
If you answered "true" to 3 or less statements – your personality is more of the monitor-evaluator or completer-finisher type.

If you are primarily a performer, you'll know in yourself that you love to do a job well, and to be admired for your performance. You need an outlet for your performing, as you tend to show off, so take up a hobby or outside interest that allows you can perform to an audience. Use your performing personality to raise morale and build team spirit.

If you are a secondary performer, the chances are that you don't have the same drive to perform as a primary performer, but you can rise to the challenge with a little coaxing. You may find this side of yourself more dominant in situations you are comfortable with, for example socially rather than at work.

If you are a monitor-evaluator or completer-finisher, you will approach situations differently (see pages 132–133 and 138–139). Play to performers' strengths by ensuring they have a prominent part to play in any event where an audience is involved. They are good at building good will and motivating a team, but can get distracted, so make sure you keep their enthusiasm in check!

ARE YOU A RESOURCE INVESTIGATOR?

Who is your favorite TV detective – Hercule Poirot? V I Warshawski? Columbo? The classic perception of private investigators is that they solve murders that have baffled the police, or spy on unfaithful spouses.

In fact, private investigation is big business, and is also used to vet potential employees, unearth corporate fraud, trace witnesses, combat internal theft, and identify forgers and counterfeiters. Private investigators must think on their feet, be adept at finding out what the situation is, and have no reservations about probing others for information. They have excellent interpersonal skills, are quite extraverted, sociable and friendly, and this approach to communication and relationships pays dividends.

Most private investigators work alone. If you transplant these investigative skills into a team or group, you get the personality type resource investigator: instead of investigating other people, these types are excellent at investigating the resources needed to get a job done. Resource investigators are highly effective when it comes to picking up ideas and making them work. They are very adaptable, and in times of imminent failure, as well as possible success, the resource investigator will turn over any and every stone in an effort to save the day.

TEST YOUR ORGANIZATIONAL SKILLS

Take a piece of paper and pen, and choose one of the following situations. Make a list of all the options you have to achieve the goal. Who would you approach? Where could you find the information you need? How would you go about things?

Organize a birthday party for 30 four-year-old children, based around the theme of transport.
Redecorate a school hall using volunteers and obtaining the materials for free.
Research a book on fun things to do in your community.

SCORING/INTERPRETATION

If you enjoyed the task and found it easy, you are primarily a resource investigator.
If you enjoyed the task a little or were just able to complete it, you are a secondary resource investigator.
If you found the task difficult, you are most likely a completer-finisher or a plant.

If you are primarily a resource investigator, you are curious and love exploring, and are a skilled negotiator. Your enthusiasm is inclined to flag if you don't get feedback, stimulation, or information from others. You enjoy a challenge, so try to stretch yourself by setting yourself a task that draws on your skills – can you raise $250 for a local charity by approaching local businesses?

If you are a secondary resource investigator, you may not have the adaptability or initial enthusiasm of a primary resource investigator, but you can still keep a project moving by pulling strings and calling in favors. You may find you are more tenacious with better staying power.

If you are a completer-finisher or a plant, you have more grounded tendencies (see pages 128–129 and 138–139). resource investigators can be overly optimistic, so ensure a dose of realism is injected where appropriate. If you have one on your team, he or she would be fantastic in any sort of fund-raising situation because this sort of person would use his or her friendliness and personal contacts to win others to the cause.

WHAT'S YOUR TOTEM ANIMAL?

The use of animal symbols is common in shamanistic cultures, particularly among the Native American and Celtic peoples, as a way of connecting with earth and nature and the power of various animals. These symbols are referred to as "totem" or "power animals." Traditionally, a totem animal is one that is with you for life. Is is usually an animal with whom you share a special connection. A power animal, on the other hand, is a spirit in animal form that comes through with a specific lesson for you.

Each totem animal represents a personality, way of behaving, or skill. We can all think of stereotypical descriptions of animals, such as owls are wise. Shamen, however, take this further. They observe the way animals live, locate food, find mates, and protect themselves, and are able to understand the particular strengths and weaknesses of each animal. In dreams and visions, shamen connect with the "manitou" of animals – the primal spirit energy of that animal type – to learn the particular lesson of that animal species. Shamen of different cultures and lands, but who share similar animal species, seem to hold similar interpretations of animal personalities and traits. For example, the mouse represents scrutiny because of the way it observes objects up close.

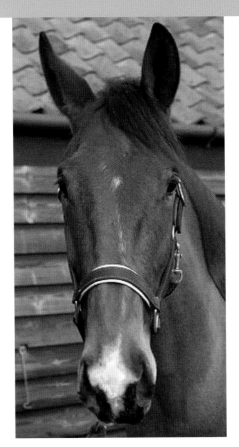

It is believed that every person has a particular *manitou*, or animal totem – sometimes more than one – to which he or she is especially attuned. For native people, these totems are generally discovered through visions, signs, or omens. If you survived an attack by a wild animal, it was believed that the animal had chosen you. In modern life, your totem animal might be shown to you by seeing a billboard with a picture of a bear, then you might come across a TV program about bears, and finally you see a cuddly teddy bear in a store window that particularly appeals to you for some reason.

Deciding how to choose your totem animal may just be a matter of looking for the right signs and interpreting them in many cases, but it can also be a therapeutic and spiritual journey, with opportunities for personal growth and self-knowledge.

In modern and urban or suburban environments, the opportunities for varied animal encounters are minimal. Instead, think about when you go to a park, forest, or zoo – what animal are you most interested in seeing? What animals are you currently interested in learning about? Which animal do you find most frightening or intriguing? Is there a recurring animal in your dreams or do you have one you have never forgotten?

Common totem animals are associated with specific personality traits:

Bear	Powerful, healing, self-sufficient, dreamer
Butterfly	Courageous, a need for change and freedom, mental powers, organized
Cat	Independent, curious, clever, loving, easily bored, unpredictable
Deer	Gentle, caring, kind, swift, intuitive, alert
Dolphin	Kind, playful, wise, realistic, trusting, good communication skills
Horse	Good stamina, loyal, friendly and cooperative, traveller
Dog	Noble, loyal, loving, respectful, enjoys serving and helping others.
Lion	Powerful, strong, patient, calm, sociable, will fight for the right cause
Rabbit	Fearful, timid, nervous, humble, prone to worrying
Wolf	Loyal, persevering, successful, courageous, strong sense of self

What can a totem animal do for you?

A totem animal can be a source of inspiration, guidance, and empowerment. It can help equip you with the knowledge and vision needed to connect more successfully with your environment. You can incorporate your totem into your life in many ways.

• Experience your totem animal in real life, by observing your animal in the wild, at a wildlife sanctuary or the zoo. Meditate on its aura and try to absorb the spiritual energy and messages it will transmit to you.

• You will be drawn to an animal for the lessons it can teach you. What aspects of its behavior are negative (in human terms)? Do you have these tendencies? You could discuss this with a friend.

• It may be possible to keep your totem animal as a pet, or to sponsor your animal at a zoo or sanctuary.

• Find a picture or sculpture of your totem animal and display it in your home or wear a replica around your neck.

ARE YOU A SHAPER?

All countries need a leader, but there are many models for achieving this. Some countries, such as the United States, combine the two roles of Head of State and Head of Government – the President of the United States is both the Head of State and the Head of Government. He has a role as the representative of America abroad, and is also the person in charge of running the country on a day-to-day basis. Another model is to split the leadership into these two roles: the Head of State may be royalty or an elected President, and a Head of Government, often called the Prime Minister. The

prime ministerial role – to run the country – is very similar to a shaper's role and personality within a team – to run a project.

Shapers are highly motivated people with a lot of nervous energy and a great need for achievement. They are outgoing and emotional, impulsive, and impatient; sometimes edgy and easily frustrated. They enjoy challenging other people and pushing them into action, but are quick to respond to challenges themselves. If obstacles arise, they will find a way round. They often have rows, but they get over them swiftly and don't harbour grudges. Headstrong and assertive, they tend to wear their emotions on their sleeve, and you'll soon know if they are disappointed or frustrated.

Shapers generally make good managers because they generate action and thrive under pressure. They are well suited to making changes and do not mind taking unpopular decisions. They are personally competitive, intolerant of vagueness and muddled thinking, and people outside the team are likely to describe them as arrogant and abrasive. Even people inside the team are in danger of being steamrollered by them on occasions, but they make things happen and deliver results.

If you are primarily a shaper, you like to lead and to push others into action, and have a lot of self-confidence. You try to achieve your objectives by whatever means possible, even if they are against the rules. You are prone to paranoia, and are sensitive about conspiracies or gossip. Interpersonal problems may arise as a result of your frustrations and criticism of others.

If you are a secondary shaper, you have some of the energy and commitment of a shaper, but are more likely to stick to rules in your pursuit of goals. You also probably have a degree more diplomacy than a primary shaper, who have few reservations about challenging or criticizing others. You are more likely to maintain a stable team.

If you are a team worker or a plant, you are probably happier being led than leading (see pages 130–131). Shapers thrive on success, results, and achieving goals. If you can break down tasks into bite sizes, you will get the best of a shaper because he or she will feel he or she is achieving something tangible and regularly.

TEST YOUR LEADERSHIP QUOTIENT

Read through this list of adjectives and descriptions.
Decide which adjective best describes either a motorcycle or a bus.

In the last column of the table, tick three adjectives that best describe you.

Description	Motorcycle/Bus	You
Speed		
Competitive		
High energy		
Aggressive		
Predictable		
Consistent		
Calm		
Inclusive		

SCORING/INTERPRETATION

Motorcycles travel at high speeds, changing lanes and routes, and have only one passenger – the driver. If you chose three "motorcycle" adjectives you are primarily a shaper.

Buses are slower, driven calmly, stick to set routes, and have room for everyone on board. If you chose three "bus" adjectives you have team worker or plant tendencies.

If you chose a mix of adjectives, you are a secondary shaper.

DO YOU WORK WELL WITH OTHERS?

Precious stones have been used in jewelry for centuries. A talented designer will mull over his or her selection, and decide how best to use them in pieces – a single gem simply set on its own, beads strung to form a necklace or bracelet, or sometimes a mix of stones grouped together. The point is that a group of different individual items (or people) can create a better impression (or perform better) as a whole.

Those of us who enjoy being part of a set or group are team workers. Team workers are sociable but not dominant. They are good communicators, trusting,

TEST YOUR PREFERENCES

Read through these questions and possible answers. For each question, choose one answer which best fits how you would choose to do things.

1. You are having some friends over for a New Year's Eve dinner. They have all offered to bring something. Do you:
a. Prefer to prepare the food yourself, so that you can plan the menu and have things the way you like them?
b. Divide up the whole meal between your friends, so that you have a pot luck party and everyone feels involved and can make a contribution?
c. Accept the offer from one or two close friends so that you can coordinate things between you?

2. It is your manager's birthday tomorrow. Do you:
a. Raise the idea of a joint card with a few people so see if anyone else thinks it's a good idea?
b. Just buy your own card so that you can decide wording that reflects your relationship?
c. Organize a card from the whole department, and get everyone to sign it?

3. You are on vacation with a large group of friends, and you have all decided to spend a day sight-seeing together. Do you:
a. Make sure you canvas everyone's opinions so that all views are fed into the final decision.
b. Sit back and let someone else make the arrangements – you're happy to go along with the group decision.
c. Take the lead in organizing a plan for the day.

sensitive, and caring. They tend to place the group's objectives and its smooth running before their own personal ambition. They aren't critical of other team members because they respect the other skills these people might bring to a group, and they endeavor to resolve infighting and interpersonal problems with a good-humored remark, a few words of praise or encouragement, or any form of input that is likely to reduce tension. The presence of a true team worker may make an enormous contribution to the team's success, simply by facilitating better cooperation among team members.

Sometimes the value of their contribution to the team goals may not be immediately obvious, but the effect of their absence is very noticeable indeed, especially in times of stress and pressure. Morale is better and people seem to cooperate better when they are around.

SCORING/INTERPRETATION

Add up your total points for all three questions as follows.

1 a. 0 b. 2 c. 1
2 a. 1 b. 0 c. 2
3 a. 2 b. 1 c. 0

If your total score was 5 or more points, you like to get everyone involved and you are primarily a team worker.
If your total score was 3 or 4 points, you are a secondary team worker.
If your total score was 2 or less points, you prefer to do things on your own, and are probably a shaper or specialist.

If you are a team worker, you are perceptive and diplomatic, sociable and concerned about others. You are good at adapting to different situations and can get along with people with whom you don't have much in common. You are likely to be indecisive in a crunch situation, since you don't like criticizing or bearing bad news. You key skill is in support-ing other people to get a job done.

If you are a secondary team worker, you may have only some of the qualities of a team worker, or exhibit them to a lesser degree. The chances are you are not quite as diplomatic, and are more likely to speak your mind if you feel that another team member is out of line.

If you are shaper or specialist, you are more likely to prefer leading than being led (see pages 146–47). Don't, however, underestimate the value of team workers. You may feel that they aren't competitive enough, but they are essential to the working of strong team. They are best at bringing parties together, so get them to organize an after-work

DO YOU FOCUS CLOSELY ON A SUBJECT?

It takes a certain type of person to become a first-class specialist. How many of us would want to dedicate ourselves to one subject, are single-minded enough to specialize our knowledge along one narrow front? There are few people who truly fit this bill.

Specialists pride themselves on acquiring technical knowledge and specialized expertise. Their priorities center on maintaining professional standards and on furthering and defending their own fields. They are indispensable in teams that rely on technical skills and a real depth of knowledge. With a team, they act as internal consultants, and command support and respect because they know more about their subjects than anyone else, and can usually be called upon to make decisions based on in-depth experience. In some teams, the lack of a specialist can cause an entire project to grind to a halt.

However, while specialists show great pride in their own subjects, they usually lack interest in those outside. They tend to dwell on technicalities rather than look for holistic solutions, and they are intolerant of generalists. Their interpersonal skills my be weak, since they prefer dealing in data or technical matters.

TEST YOUR APPROACH TO FUNDAMENTALS

The basis of religion can be used to generalize aspects of personality. While most of the major world religions are monotheistic – they involve the worship of one God – some hold that God may take more than one form, and that each form has a special and specialized role to play. Think about your attitude toward your work and colleagues and decide which religion is closest to your beliefs in this part of your life.

Judaism

There is a single, all-powerful God, who created the universe and everything in it, and God has a special relationship with his people. The fundamental beliefs of Judaism are those cemented by the covenant that God made with Moses on Mount Sinai, more than 3500 years ago.

If you are a specialist, you feel most comfortable in your own niche, with a relatively narrow but deep knowledge base – think Grand Canyon! You expect other people to specialize, too, and find generalists somewhat woolly-thinking. Make sure you don't miss the bigger picture by focusing too hard on your pet subject.

If you are a secondary specialist, the chances are that you can act as a specialist in a number of areas – you haven't centered all your efforts on just one topic. The advantages of this approach are that you have a wider knowledge base, but be wary of thinking you know it all; compared to a primary specialist you are just an amateur!

If you are a team worker or performer, you have a more generalist approach to life (see pages 140–141 and 148–149). Specialists can be essential members of a team but are prone to going their own ways and not really becoming part of the team spirit, so make sure they are included whenever possible and encourage their contributions on a wide range of topics.

Christianity

There is only one God, but he reveals himself in three "persons" – Father, Son (Jesus Christ), and Holy Spirit – who are regarded as a unity. The basis of Christianity is humans are created at a distance from God and are responsible for their own lives.

Hinduism

There are many gods and goddesses, but these are all aspects of the one supreme God or spirit, Brahman. For example, the gods Vishnu, Shiva, and Brahma are different forms of Brahman: Brahma reflects God's divine work of creating the universe, Vishnu reflects God's work in keeping the universe in existence, and Shiva reflects God's work in destroying it.

SCORING/INTERPRETATION

Which of these religious approaches best reflects your views?

If you chose Judaism, you feel it's better to have a little knowledge of everything, and prefer to take a generalist approach. You are probably a team worker or performer.

If you chose Christianity, you feel that a degree of specialization can be beneficial, but that in the end generalism pays off. You are a secondary specialist.

If you chose Hinduism, you see the great advantages to specializing, and you feel more comfortable when everyone has a distinct job or role. You are primarily a specialist.

YOUR EXTERNAL TYPE PROFILE

If you've completed all the external type tests, you can profile your results to get an overall view of your external personality, which will help you understand your relationships with other people, and your natural preference for interaction with others. Circle the relevant boxes for each of your test scores, then add up the circled items you have in each column.

	A	B	C
Pages 128–129	Plant	Secondary Plant	Implementer or Specialist
Pages 130–131	Coordinator	Secondary Coordinator	Implementer or Specialist
Pages 132–133	Coordinator, Performer	Secondary Monitor-Evaluator	Monitor-Evaluator
Pages 136–137	Plant or Resource Investigator	Secondary Implementer	Implementer
Pages 138–139	Coordinator, Implementer	Secondary Completer Finisher	Completer Finisher
Pages 140–141	Performer	Secondary Performer	Monitor-Evaluator, Completer Finisher
Pages 142–143	Resource Investigator	Secondary Resource Investigator	Completer Finisher, Plant
Pages 146–147	Team Worker, Plant	Secondary Shaper	Shaper
Pages 148–149	Team Worker	Secondary Team Worker	Shaper, Specialist
Pages 150–151	Team Worker, Performer	Secondary Specialist	Specialist

Total number

SCORING

If you have the most circled items in Column A, you are spontaneous.

If you have the most circled items in Column B or an equal number of circled items in any two columns, you are methodical.

If you have the most circled items in Column C, you are rule respectful.

INTERPRETATION

Spontaneous

You enjoy getting the best out of people, and use your personality to raise morale and build team spirit. You are a natural diplomat, good at adapting to different situations, and getting along with people with whom you don't necessarily have much in common. You are curious and dislike constraints, and tackle problems calmly and effectively. Your hobbies and interests reflect your creativity and imagination.

However, you are likely to be indecisive in a crunch situation, because you don't like criticizing people or bearing bad news. Your enthusiasm is inclined to flag if you don't get feedback or stimulation from others. There is a lazy side to your personality, and you have a tendency to get someone else to do your work.

Rule respectful

You are intelligent, discerning, and objective, and respected for your sound judgment. You enjoy working through tasks logically, and stick to rules, formulas, and guidelines, creating them where they don't already exist. You are good at picking up the loose ends of projects because you are tenacious and organized, with an eye for detail, and will doggedly see things through to the bitter end.

However, you can have a propensity for paranoia, and sensitivity about conspiracies or gossip. Interpersonal problems may arise through your frustrations and criticism of other people's work or working styles. You tend to keep your emotions in check, and can come across as rather cool and arrogant. Sometimes you miss the bigger picture by getting carried away with your own pet projects and seeing events only from your own perspective.

Methodical

You enjoy being part of the planning process, but are able to work comfortably in a more chaotic environment. You like to stick to rules in your pursuit of goals, and aim to "get the job done," keeping a project moving by pulling strings and calling in favors. You can rise to the challenge with a little coaxing, and may grab opportunities if they come your way. Your friends and the friendship of colleagues are important to you.

Your weak spots are your lack of adaptability: You feel uncomfortable with breaking rules for the sake of expediency or the greater good. You are a relatively conventional person, and tend to go with the flow rather than take "the road less traveled." You are likely to speak your mind if you feel that another team member is out of line, and this verbal bluntness may make you unpopular.

PERSONALITY TESTS IN RECRUITMENT

Most organizations, from huge corporations and independent charities to healthcare providers and schools, now put potential recruits through a range of tests as part of their selection process. For graduate programs, this might involve attending an assessment center, often run over one or two days, completing case studies, negotiation exercises, and team challenges. Gruelling one-to-one interviews may test technical knowledge or experience. In addition, psychometric testing is often used to test numerical and verbal aptitude, and personality.

Many small employers, too, now use psychometric testing to assess the personalities of potential employees. There are several kinds of test but usually candidates have to answer questions on their preferences and interests. Their answers provide information about their natural way of working, and aim to predict how they will get on with colleagues.

Are tests fair?

Various research studies have shown that most people are rather cynical about personality questionnaires, partly because they can't see how their personality can be measured by a few questions, and partly because they find it hard to see the value of revealing personal thoughts and feelings at a job interview.

It is estimated that there are 2500 personality tests available to organizations; some are of higher quality that others. Professional psychometric tests are restricted to those with appropriate training to administer and interpret them, and have to pass rigorous quality controls to ensure they are testing what they say they are, and that they aren't discriminating on gender or race. The best tests actually do produce a reasonably accurate profile about the candidate's character and, therefore, how he or she is likely to behave at work. They have the added advantage of providing a level playing field, too, so that any individual interviewer's bias is tempered by some cool, hard data.

As a job-hunter, you have the right to know what your prospective employer is assessing, the qualifications of the assessor, and whether there will be an opportunity to discuss the results. Your answers are essentially your property, which you are sharing with the employer, and you should have the results explained to you. Psychometric tests should only be one part of the recruitment process and employers should spend at least 15 minutes elaborating on the test results. Feedback is crucial.

Can I fake it?

The answer is "yes," of course you can, just as you can pretend to be someone you are not at interview, or embellish your resumé with fantastic achievements. But you would have to second-guess the personality the employer wants, which is not always as simple as you might think. And many of the better tests have in-built "impression management" profiles, which look at whether you are trying to fake-good, fake-bad or just simply fake it. There are a variety of devices for catching fakers out, including:

• The same question is asked in a variety of different ways at different points in the questionnaire and the scoring looks for major discrepancies. If you do have this quality in your personality, you'll answer consistently.

• The candidate has to choose between two "unattractive" personality features, such as "I am quick-tempered" and "I get frustrated if I don't do things my way." This forces you to admit to aspects of your personality you might want to keep hidden.

• Some questions sound bad, but in fact are representative of most people. "I have told a lie at work" may be answered "never" by someone trying to fake-good, whereas in reality practically everyone has told a lie once for some reason.

So if you are given a test at interview, don't be tempted to fill in the answers you think the interviewer is looking for. If you're too perfect, they'll smell a rat. And if you have to misrepresent yourself, is it really the job for you? If you get the job you will be storing up problems because there could be things you won't want or be able to do.

What should I do when taking tests?

Basically, stay relaxed and be yourself. Here's some general advice:

• Be prepared. Get a good night's sleep and arrive in plenty of time, so that you're physically and mentally ready to sit the test.

• Be curious. Make sure you're absolutely clear about the testing process and what it will involve. Don't be afraid to ask questions.

• Be confident. There are no right and wrong answers. Have faith in yourself and answer how you see fit.

• Be yourself. It's easy to lie but, if you're not true to yourself, you're more likely to be rumbled in the interview. It's best to be honest.

• Be realistic. Remember that these tests are designed to find a very specific person. If you're not selected, it doesn't mean there's something wrong with your personality – you just weren't the personality they were looking for. That could well be to your benefit, too.

• Get feedback. Organizations should give you feedback on your test – use this constructively to think realistically about your job search.

So you've taken a whole heap of psychometric tests, including a personality test, and you got the job. No more testing, right? Wrong! You are likely to find now, particularly in larger organizations, that the tests keep on coming. There are three other uses of personality tests: career development (advice on what future jobs would be right for you), selection (to check your profile and preferences for a job promotion), and team-building (to put together teams with the right dynamics for success).

Career development

There are two angles on career development. Large organizations and institutions often run special recruitment programs, where they fast-track talented individuals who are ear-marked as future senior managers. A common starting point is to spend time in every department, getting a feel for the organization and its issues. Recruits are then invited to state their preferred specialty, such as sales or finance, and various psychometric tests are completed to aid this decision. It is common for the results to be fed back quite openly with the test-taker, and a discussion will result in the recruit's future placement and career path. Some organizations repeat this process at regular intervals. The whole process is generally quite benign and non-threatening.

Career development counseling, including personality testing, is often offered after redundancy, and gives the test-taker a chance to step off the treadmill and evaluate his or her strengths and weaknesses in terms of possible careers. Many people find themselves following a career path more from luck than judgment, and personality tests offer objectivity. Together with an evaluation of a person's lifestyle and values, this process can lead to better job satisfaction and personal fulfilment. The benefits are such that career development counseling is commonly sought by people looking for a change in direction or lifestyle.

Selection

Imagine you've been in your current role for two or three years. You are looking to climb the next rung on the ladder of career success and acquire more responsibility and the opportunity to develop new skills. Your boss announces she is leaving, or you see a new position advertised on the notice board at work. You apply, are invited for interview, and you are asked to take a personality test – again!

The same rules apply for answering honestly, in fact, it is even more critical to be yourself, since your employers have your previous profile on record. Make sure you have a copy of the job specification in advance, and think about the sort of person who would be good at this role. Do you have what it takes? You should know your human resources department well by now, and are just as entitled to feedback as if you were a new recruit.

Team building

Team building has been recognized by many companies as an important factor in providing a quality service and remaining competitive. There are very few jobs now which do not have a team element, yet there are some teams whose collective performance falls short of what you might expect given the quality of individuals. Team structures are often complicated; people can be members of several teams, the team may be temporary and project-based, or a permanent fixture. Teams as a way of working are here to stay.

We can define a team as "a group of people working toward a common goal," and "team building" as the process of enabling that group of people to reach their goals. One of the biggest factors that can stand in its way is personality. We've all tried to work with people who were bossy, lazy, uncommitted, divisive, and inflexible – the same people are often great at their job, but in combination with the wrong personality, the team goes belly up. This is where personality tests come in – as a way of identifying team roles, predicting successful working relationships ,and avoiding potentially wasteful personality clashes. Personality testing has become a routine part of corporate life.

INDEX

The author would like to thank:
Chris, for his encouragement and support
Beth, for her love and laughter
Charlie, for getting me out when I needed a break
Haw Park Farm, for being in the right place at the right time...
And the dedicated and talented team at Carroll & Brown

Carroll & Brown would like to thank:
Design Emily Cook, Laura de Grasse
Photography Jules Selmes, David Yems
Illustration Jurgen Ziewe, Juliet Percival, Wendy Andrew, Simone Boni, Oliver Burston/www.debutart.com, Alison Barratt/www.thorogood.net
IT Management Paul Stradling
Picture Research Sandra Schneider

Picture Credits:
page 10 Getty Images
page 16-17 Reuters/Corbis
page 18 Getty Images
page 25 (center) Mary Evans/Charles Folkard
page 28 (bottom left) Cole and Son/www.fabricsandwallpapers.com; (bottom right) Lewis and Wood/www.fabricsandwallpapers.com
page 29 Hoople Collection from CWV Group Ltd/www.wallpaperdirect.com
page 30 Charles D Winters/SPL
page 32 Bettmann/Corbis
page 34-5 Garden Picture Library/Jason Ingram
page 36 Touchstone/The Kobal Collection/Marks,Elliott
page 37 Orion/The Kobal Collection/Lamana-Wills,Gemma
page 40 Mary Evans Picture Library
page 42 (top left, bottom right) Getty Images
page 48 Mark Garlick/SPL
page 50 (blue flower) Claude Nuridsany and Marie Perennou/SPL
page 52 (left) World Religions Photolibrary
page 55 Thomas Schweizer/Corbis
page 56 National Geographic/Getty Images
page 57 Peter Chadwick/SPL
page 60 Mary Evans/Charles Folkard
page 67 (center) Art Wolfe/SPL
page 68 Getty Images
page 78 Art Wolfe/SPL
page 80 Getty Images
page 84 Mary Evans Picture Library
page 92 (left) Tim Davis/SPL; (right) Peter Chadwick/SPL
page 98 (center) Scott Camazine/SPL; (right) Getty Images
page 99 (center) Getty Images
page 100 Bettmann/Corbis
page 102-3 Georgina Cranston/Office of Tibet, London
page 106 Getty Images
page 108 Getty Images
page 110 (top) Getty Images; (bottom) Bettmann/Corbis
page 112 (top) Scott Camazine/SPL; (bottom) Sinclair Stammers/SPL
page 113 James H Robinson/SPL
page 116 Keystone/Rex Features
page 118 (bottom) Peter Chadwick/SPL
page 120 (left) Getty Images
page 127 (center) Getty Images
page 132 Getty Images
page 136 Hufton and Crow/View/Romy and John Skok
page 136/7 Glas Architects
page 146 Triumph Speed Triple courtesy of Triumph Motorcycles Limited
page 150 Getty Images